BIBLE
PROPHECY:
The
ESSENTIALS

BIBLE PROPHECY: *The* ESSENTIALS

AMIR TSARFATI & BARRY STAGNER

HARVEST PROPHECY
AN IMPRINT OF HARVEST HOUSE PUBLISHERS

Cover design by Bryce Williamson

Cover photo © ninell / Adobe Stock; kyoshino, Roberto, DNY59 / Gettyimages

Interior design by Aesthetic Soup

For bulk, special sales, or ministry purchases, please call 1-800-547-8979. Email: Customerservice@hhpbooks.com

Bible Prophecy: The Essentials
Copyright © 2022 by Amir Tsarfati and Barry Stagner
Published by Harvest House Publishers
Eugene, Oregon 97408
www.harvesthousepublishers.com

ISBN 978-0-7369-8724-0 (pbk)
ISBN 978-0-7369-8725-7 (eBook)

Library of Congress Control Number: 2022939439

Printed in the United States of America

22 23 24 25 26 27 28 29 30 / BP / 10 9 8 7 6 5 4 3 2 1

From Amir:
To my father-in-law, Hanan.
You always had the right answers to my questions.
You are loved, and you are greatly missed.

From Barry:
To my loving and incredibly supportive wife, Teri.

Many thanks to Pastor Mike Golay
for navigating the online
question-and-answer broadcasts
from which these questions are derived.
Your hard work and insights
are much appreciated!

CONTENTS

WE LIVE IN PERILOUS TIMES

In the midst of the perilous times in which we live—a time of false Christs, wars and rumors of wars, ethnic tensions, famines, pestilences, and earthquakes all increasing in a labor-pain-like progression—we need to remember that we are living during a very privileged season of church history.

In Daniel 12:4, the prophet was told to seal up the book until the time of the end. And today, we live in that time, during which what Daniel—and other prophets like Ezekiel, Jeremiah, and Isaiah—wrote is no longer sealed or shut up from our understanding. While we are living in an era of unprecedented prophetic activity and clarity, there are still questions many people have regarding Bible prophecy.

In this book, we have compiled 70 frequently asked questions from the live Q&A sessions we have been doing for the past couple of years. We are hoping this format provides you with a useful go-to resource for not only finding answers to questions about Bible prophecy, but equipping you to be able to share those answers with others.

As you read, may "the LORD bless you and keep you; the LORD make His face shine upon you, and be gracious to you; the LORD lift up His countenance upon you, and give you peace" (Numbers 6:24-26).

Even so, come quickly, Lord Jesus!

Love and blessings to you,
Amir and Barry

CHAPTER 1

ISRAEL

ISRAEL

A mong God's most amazing miracles of all time is His preservation of the nation of Israel. Not long after Jesus' crucifixion, resurrection, and ascension to heaven, the Roman Empire sent armies to destroy Jerusalem and the temple, and the Jewish people were scattered abroad to the nations. For many centuries, the land was ruled by hostile foreign powers.

But beginning in the late nineteenth century, God worked in numerous ways through people and events to restore Israel as a nation. Jewish people began to return to the land, with their numbers increasing up through World War II, especially as Jews fled Europe during the Holocaust.

Then on May 14, 1948, the modern State of Israel was born. On a live radio broadcast, the first prime minister of Israel, David Ben-Gurion, read aloud the words of Israel's Declaration of Independence. Those who were familiar with Bible prophecy recognized the significance of what was happening. Time and again, the prophets had predicted that there would come a day when the Jewish people returned to the Holy Land, and, at last, it was now happening. As God promised in Ezekiel 36:8-10:

> You, O mountains of Israel, you shall shoot forth your branches and yield your fruit to My people Israel, for they are about to come. For indeed I am for you, and I will turn to you, and you shall be tilled and sown. I will multiply men upon you, all the house of Israel, all of it; and the cities shall be inhabited and the ruins rebuilt.

Here we see God speaking fertility into this dead land in preparation for the masses of Jewish people who would return. And today, the land is bountiful and filled with life. God has brought back His people by air, on ships, and by land. This is not man's doing, but God's. Against all odds, the nation of Israel has returned to its homeland and prospered.

The fact Israel is a country today—after 2,000 years of the Jewish people having been scattered worldwide—confirms God is faithful to His promises. And just as He has been faithful to Israel, He will be faithful to us. He will fulfill His promise in John 14:1-3 to rapture us and take us to be with Him in heaven. It is because God is faithful that we can have hope, and that we can be certain about the wonderful future that awaits us.[1]

1. Did God choose the nation of Israel or just the man Jacob?

Amir: The answer is simple: Jacob *is* Israel. When Jacob wrestled with the Lord in Genesis 32, the Lord changed his name to Israel. Also, all throughout Scripture, the tribes of Israel are called the sons of Jacob. Yes, God chose Jacob, and that is the same as choosing Israel.

The promises made to Israel were not for only one person, but for the whole nation. In the Bible, sometimes the nation of Israel is referred to as Jacob, and vice versa. You cannot separate them. The Lord said through the prophet Malachi, "I am the LORD, I do not change; therefore you are not consumed, O sons of Jacob" (3:6). Even though since their early days the Israelites had drifted away from the Lord's ordinances, God Himself confirmed that Jacob is national Israel.

Barry: When God made His covenant promises with national Israel, He also made promises regarding the land of Israel. In Genesis 17:8, the Lord said He was giving the land of Canaan to the descendants of Abraham through Isaac and Jacob—and not through Ishmael—as an everlasting possession. So not only did God choose the nation of Israel, He also chose the land that would become their national home.

Why would God give all the land of Canaan to one man? He didn't—He gave the land as an everlasting possession to the Jewish people. In case you've wondered, the people of Israel began to be referred to as the Jews after the Babylonian captivity because the majority of the captives were from Judah. Today, not all Israelis are Jews in the sense of geographic homeland, but in a spiritual sense. The Jews, Israel, and Jacob are all references to the same people group, not a single individual.

2. Is the rebirth of Israel important to Bible prophecy?

Amir: Most definitely yes! God promised that in the latter days, He would bring His people back into the land. He said through the prophets that Israel's banishment from the land was temporary and that He would bring the people back because He promised the land to the descendants of Abraham through Isaac and Jacob. In Jeremiah 31:35-36, the Lord said that when the sun, moon, and stars stop giving their light, then you will know that Israel is no longer a nation in His eyes.

We also know from Zechariah 12:10 that God has brought His people back into the land because He is going to save them. A time is coming when they will "look on [Him] whom they pierced," and "they will mourn for Him as one mourns for his only son, and grieve for Him as one grieves for a firstborn."

We also know that in the future, there must be a third temple on the Temple Mount so that the antichrist can commit the abomination of desolation. For that to happen, Israel must be in possession of all of Jerusalem, including the Temple Mount. The prophet Amos said that when Israel comes back into the land, the people will never be uprooted from it (Amos 9:14-15), and we have seen this be fulfilled. Israel has been attacked repeatedly since it became a nation in 1948, and yet the mighty hand of God has been a strong tower for His people and protected them.

Israel must be back in the land for all these things to happen.

Barry: I would say the rebirth of the nation of Israel is probably the most important sign of the last days. It set the stage for the end of the time of the Gentiles (Luke 21:24), which will conclude with the rapture of the church and opens the door for the seventieth week of Daniel to be fulfilled.

Israel has been referred to by prophecy teachers as God's timepiece. You cannot understand last days if you do not see Israel as central to that time period. In fact, the rebirth of Israel and the regathering of the Jews back into their national homeland are integral to the integrity of Scripture. If the modern nation of Israel has nothing to do with the Israel of the Bible, then passages like Amos 9:14-15 are either unfulfilled, allegorical, or untrue. Any of those interpretive approaches to the prophecies concerning the nation of Israel cause major problems for the other prophetic passages in Scripture. What does it mean for someone to make a covenant for seven years and then break it at the midpoint (Daniel 9:27)? What allegorical application can you derive from that? What is the abomination of desolation that Jesus spoke of that requires a Jewish temple in Jerusalem (Matthew 24:15)? The list goes on and on. Thus, the presence of the modern state of Israel is essential to interpreting all prophecies concerning the last days.

The most significant of all the reasons that modern Israel is a fulfillment of prophecy is what we are told in Daniel 9:24: "Seventy weeks are determined for your people and for your holy city." We can now look back and see the three divisions of the 70 weeks happen exactly as they were described in Scripture. The word "weeks" actually means "sevens," and we see that there are 70 "sevens" determined for Daniel's people, the Jews, and the holy city, Jerusalem. We can see that the sevens are periods of seven years, and Daniel was told they would occur in three parts: seven weeks, then 62 weeks, then one week—with that final week being the seventieth.

The first seven weeks refer to the time from Artaxerxes's decree for the Jewish people to return to their land to when they rebuilt Jerusalem. The next 62 weeks spanned the time from the rebuilding of Jerusalem to the day of Jesus' triumphal entry, when He rode into Jerusalem on a donkey and was recognized as the one who came in the name of the Lord. If the first seven weeks had a literal fulfillment and the next 62 weeks also had a literal fulfillment, then the seventieth week must also have a literal fulfillment.

Israel is God's timepiece, and the rebirth of the nation began the march toward the seventieth week of Daniel—or the tribulation—which has yet to be fulfilled.

3. What did Paul mean when he said "all Israel will be saved" in Romans 11:26?

Barry: Let's look at the bigger context first. In Romans chapter 11, the apostle Paul wrote about God's temporary rejection of national Israel. He posed this question in verse 1: "Has God cast away His people?" He then answered with an emphatic "Certainly not!" Later in the chapter, Paul taught about the grafting in of the Gentile branches to the root of the Jews. This implies that the root is necessary for the existence of the branches, or the predominantly Gentile church.

Paul then said that this blindness, in part, has happened to the Jews until the fullness of the Gentiles has come in—then all Israel will be saved (verses 25-26). This tells us that after the church age, which will end when the rapture takes place, all Israel will be saved—that is, during the tribulation. That's the wonderful news. The sad part is that according to Zechariah 14:8, two-thirds of the Jews will die during the tribulation, and the remaining one-third (that constitutes all Israel) will be saved.

Again, this underscores the necessity of there being an Israel for "all Israel" to be saved. The covenant people who were promised a Holy One who would save them, as stated in Zechariah 9:16, have yet to see this fulfilled. But with the Jews back in their national homeland and in possession of their capital city, this is possible.

Amir: It is a tragic that two-thirds of Israel will die in unbelief during the tribulation in much the same way that the generation that made the exodus out of Egypt died in the wilderness in unbelief. This also reminds us that there is but one Savior of the Jews and the Gentiles, and that is our Lord Yeshua, who came to the Jews first, through whom the Messiah came into the world.

Like the apostle Paul, I have a great burden for my countrymen (Romans 9:1-5), desiring that they would come to know the Holy One of Israel as their Savior. But I also know that it is their suffering that Zechariah speaks of that will lead them to the place where they finally see that the One who was wounded for their transgressions and bruised for their iniquities is the One whom they rejected and pierced.

In Zechariah 13:9, God said, "I will bring the one-third through the fire, will refine them as silver is refined, and test them as gold is tested. They will call on My name, and I will answer them. I will say, 'This is My people'; and each one will say, 'The LORD is my God.'"

The one-third who will go "through the fire" are the Jewish people Paul spoke of in Romans 11:26 when he wrote that "all Israel will be saved."

4. Are the annexation efforts in Israel today found in Bible prophecy?

Amir: First, we must keep in mind that the return of the Jews to their land was prophesied. The Lord promised this through the major and the minor prophets, including in Ezekiel chapters 36–37. The fact Israel is in the land again is why we believe that the events of Ezekiel 38–39 are around the corner. God gave this land to the Jews and said He would bring them back, and that includes the Jewish possession of Jerusalem.

Because of God's promises, there is absolutely nothing unbiblical about having parts of the land of Israel—the ancestral homeland of the Jewish people—being declared as belonging to the state of Israel. This is biblical. I personally don't see any problem with the annexation efforts. In fact, I watched an interview recently with a Saudi journalist who said, "I believe that the Israelis should move ahead with annexation."

The Palestinians have had multiple opportunities to get whatever land they needed, and they missed all of them. The world needs to face the reality that Israel is a sovereign nation, and all of Israel is sovereign Israeli territory. Some of the Arab states today are favoring Israel in the Middle East conflict simply because Israel is now important to them in the fight against Iran.

Bible prophecy said the Jewish people would come back into their land—all of it. One of the positive results of the pandemic and the ethnic tensions and riots around the world is that they have spurred a remarkable interest among Jews worldwide to move to Israel. Recently, the Israeli government has received immigration inquiries from more than a quarter of a million Jews from America, Australia, France, Germany, and other places.

While the annexation efforts are not *directly* related to a specific Bible prophecy, they fit within God's prophetic promises to bring the Jewish people back to their homeland.

Barry: The fact that the annexation efforts most often in question are biblical Judea and Samaria—called the West Bank by many today—indicates these regions are part of God's promised homeland for the Jews. That's why it is important for Christians to recognize these areas as being part of Israel.

Jerusalem is the eternal capital of Israel, and there's no way to come to any other conclusion after a careful study of Scripture—especially the prophetic portions of Ezekiel and Zechariah. These prophets were clear about the geography of last days and the return of the Jewish people to the land that God had given them.

As Amir said, because of all the chaos happening in the world, Jews who live all over the globe are saying, "Maybe it's time to go home." The Bible said this would happen, and we've seen this immigration taking place for more than 100 years. With the recent major push for the Jewish people to make *aliyah* ("ascent to Israel"), we cannot help but realize we are getting closer to the seventieth week of Daniel. The concerns people are expressing about Israel's annexation of Judea and Samaria may have prophetic significance in connection with the prophecy about Israel becoming an increasingly burdensome stone to the international community (Zechariah 12:3).

5. Where are the lost tribes of Israel, and which tribes are currently in Israel today?

Barry: The short answer is that all of them are now in Israel—none are lost. The rest of the answer is that when people talk about the "lost tribes," usually they are referring to the ten tribes of the northern kingdom of Israel, who were taken captive and carried away by the Assyrians. British Israelism erringly teaches that Anglo-Saxons are actually the Jews, and Mormons believe they descended from Ephraim and Manasseh. Both views are incorrect. The reality is that the idea of lost tribes is a misnomer. God doesn't lose track of anything, including who and where His chosen people are. He knows exactly where they are, and He has been gathering them back into their homeland for more than a century. If God were to lose track of anyone or anything, we would have great reason for concern. But thankfully, that isn't the case.

We should also keep in mind the multitude of instructions God gave to Israel, forbidding His people to intermarry with those from other nations. He wanted them to maintain their national identity and practices, which distinguished them from other peoples of the world. Looking back, we can now see how important this was. Through the ages, pockets of Jews scattered all across the globe maintained their Jewish identity and kept meticulous records of their ancestry. This allowed them, over the past 2,000 years, to maintain their national identity even though they did not have a nation to call their home until 1948.

Virtually all other ancient cultures that were captured or driven from their homelands were assimilated into the cultures and nations that conquered them. The only exception is God's chosen people. By maintaining their identity, their future homecoming became possible.

Amir: I believe that all the tribes are out there, and that predominately it's the tribe of Judah and the Levites (with the surname Cohen) that are back in the land right now. However, God is bringing back people from the tribes of Dan and Manasseh. We are seeing Jewish people who are not from the tribe of Judah come back from the diaspora from places like India, Ethiopia, and other countries in Asia and Africa.

We know the 12 tribes still exist because according to Ezekiel, during the millennial kingdom, the land will again be divided by tribes. All the tribes will receive an inheritance, and Joseph will be given a double portion. Ezekiel 48:29 says, "This is the land which you shall divide by lot as an inheritance among the tribes of Israel." We know the context of this passage is the millennium because Ezekiel 40–48 gives exhaustive and specific details about that era—a time during which healing waters will flow from the threshold of the temple, according to Ezekiel 47:1. These healing waters are consistent with what Zechariah 14:8 records about the return of Jesus to the Mount of Olives and the "living waters" flowing from Jerusalem and bringing life back to the Dead Sea.

Every tribe is named in Ezekiel 48, as arc two of Joseph's sons, Ephraim and Manasseh. And specific geographic boundaries are listed in that chapter, which again requires every tribe's presence at that time.

6. Do the blessings and curses of Genesis 12:3 still apply today?

Amir: Yes. God promised that through Abraham, all the families of the earth would be blessed. That means families today are still being blessed through Abraham. In what way? Through the One who came from Abraham's grandson Jacob, who had 12 sons, including one named Judah. Through the lineage of Judah—the tribe of kings—came the Messiah, Yeshua, who is still a blessing to people today. If the blessings part is still true, then the curses part also has to be true. Remember, Jacob was renamed Israel, the Jews are the chosen people of God, and land was given to God's chosen people as an eternal inheritance.

Look at how God has brought His people back into the land as He promised, and how He has protected them through the many times they have been attacked since 1948. The plans of Israel's enemies have been cursed. On the very day the Jewish people declared themselves to be a nation again, they were attacked by five Arab nations with trained armies, guns, tanks, and planes. Their goal was to wipe out Israel right from the start. What was the outcome of that war? Behold Israel today, and you will see. The enemies who attacked did not prevail, nor did they in 1967 or 1973. They could not prevail because those who curse Israel will themselves be cursed. Yes, Genesis 12:3 is still in effect today.

Barry: Amen! The key word in this promise is "all," which, as Amir pointed out, gives us the scope and duration of God's promise. Genesis 12:3 declares that through Abraham "*all* the families of the earth shall be blessed."

One interesting aspect of this promise is that when the Lord said, "Whoever curses you I will curse," He used two different Hebrew words that are both translated "curse" or "curses." The first Hebrew word means "to trouble," and the second means "to lightly esteem," or to "think little or nothing of." That means the Lord will trouble those who think little or nothing of Israel.

This is one of many reasons that Replacement Theology is so dangerous and heretical. As Amir pointed out, if the positive part of the promise is still true, then the negative part must be true as well. God has promised to trouble those who think little or nothing of His chosen people—through whom He would send the One who would be a blessing to all the families of the earth.

Yet additional evidence that confirms the negative part of Genesis 12:3 is still true is a prophecy that appears in Zechariah 12:3, which describes what will happen during the tribulation period. There, we read that those who come against the Jews "will surely be cut in pieces."

Back when Hamas terrorists in the Gaza Strip attacked Israel in 2014, they complained, "Their God changes the paths of our rockets in mid-air."[2] They might be right! God is for Israel, and He who watches over Israel "shall neither slumber nor sleep" (Psalm 121:4).

When you mess with the people of Israel, you are messing with the God of Israel. Genesis 12:3 is still true today.

7. **What is meant by "the day of the Lord"? Is that a literal 24-hour period? Or is it an era or season like the days of Noah?**

Amir: Most of the Bible's descriptions of the day of the Lord refer to a time of terrible trial that will come upon sinners who remain on earth after the rapture of the church. You definitely want to avoid this day, which can be done only by accepting Christ as your Savior. In other words, the day of the Lord is the time when He will pour out His judgments on earth.

This is why we know the day of the Lord has not started yet. The antichrist has not emerged on the scene, and his rise to power is what will mark the beginning of the seventieth week of Daniel, or the start of the seven-year tribulation.

The believers at Thessalonica didn't understand this. Some people had told them the seventieth week of Daniel had already begun, based on what Paul said in 2 Thessalonians 2:2. Someone may have even taught this and forged Paul's signature on a letter that they claimed was from him. Paul said, "Don't believe anyone—not even someone who claims to speak in my name or bear my signature—who tells you that the day of the Lord has come."

The day of the Lord, or the seven-year tribulation, will be a time unlike any other. In Malachi 4:5, it is described as "the great and dreadful day of the LORD." It's definitely not a 24-hour period, just like the "week" in Daniel 9:24-27 is not seven days but seven years. While the Bible uses the term "the day of the LORD" to describe this time frame, it clearly does not refer to a 24-hour day. Rather, it points to the seven years of tribulation that will come upon this world, and Israel will go through it. The church will not face the tribulation because it is not destined to endure the wrath of God. Believers will be "caught up" (1 Thessalonians 4:17) in a moment, in the twinkling of an eye (1 Corinthians 15:52). The church will be *delivered from* and not *preserved through* "the hour of trial which shall come upon the whole world," as Jesus said in Revelation 3:10.

Barry: Zechariah chapters 12–14 describe the tribulation from beginning to end. Sixteen times in those chapters, Zechariah uses the phrase "in that day" to describe the seventieth week of Daniel or the tribulation. The day the prophet is referring to is the day of the Lord. It starts with Jerusalem becoming a burdensome stone to all the nations and ends with the Jews looking upon the One whom they pierced and mourning for Him as one mourns for an only Son. This will happen at the end of the day of the Lord, when Jesus comes back and descends upon the Mount of Olives.

Jesus said the entire time will be "such as has not been since the beginning of the world until this time, no, nor ever shall be" (Matthew 24:21). During this time, God will discipline His chosen people of Israel, and at the end, all Israel will be saved (Romans 11:26). Zechariah 13:8 informs us that two-thirds of the Jews will die during the tribulation, and the remaining one-third—which will constitute believing Israel—will look upon Jesus and become saved, recognizing Him at last for who He truly is: the Holy One of Israel, their Savior.

The phrase *the day of the Lord* is a figure of speech, much like when someone says, "Your day will come," which usually means that eventually, you will get what you deserve. This is what the day of the Lord is: the Christ-rejecting world will experience the wrath of God for seven years, until finally, as Revelation 15:1 says, "the wrath of God is complete." The day of the Lord is synonymous with the seventieth week of Daniel, the tribulation, and "the time of Jacob's trouble" (Jeremiah 30:7). They all speak of seven years of unparalleled cataclysmic disasters one after the other until the final rebellion takes place—at which time Jesus will return and defeat, with the breath of His mouth, the armies gathered against Jerusalem. Then the Prince of Peace will rule the world. A thousand years later, Satan will be released and deceive the nations and gather them for one final battle against the Lord, before eternity begins.

8. Some say the Jews are saved by keeping the law, and Gentiles are saved by believing the gospel. Is this true?

Barry: This is called Dual Covenant Theology, and it is absolute heresy. It is sad to know that so many who claim to love Israel teach and believe this, as it denies the only means by which anyone can be saved: through belief in Jesus Christ as Savior and Lord. For a Christian to tell Jewish people that they don't need to come to faith in Christ for salvation but that they can be saved by keeping the law is to condemn them to hell. There is nothing in the 613 precepts and ordinances of the Mosaic law that indicates the law can save anyone. The law, including the observances and feast days of the Jews, was meant to distinguish God's people from the world, not save their perishing souls.

That's why the conversation Jesus had with Nicodemus in John chapter 3 is so important. Jesus acknowledged that Nicodemus was "the teacher of Israel," indicating he was a prominent rabbi. Yet when Nicodemus asked how a person could be born again, Jesus replied, "Are you the teacher of Israel, and do not know these things?" (verse 10). Jesus was saying, "As someone under the law, didn't you learn that you fall short—that you are a lawbreaker and therefore you are a sinner?" The purpose of the law was to make it clear that no one could measure up to God's standard. To say that the Jews can be saved by keeping the law condemns them. The Jews need a Savior just like everyone else, and there is only one Savior: Christ the Lord, the King of the Jews and the head of the church.

Amir: If the Jews can be saved by keeping the law, why was Paul always pleading with them to come to Christ as Savior? Why did he first go to the synagogue in every city to preach Christ and Him crucified? Why didn't he go to every city during his travels and teach the precepts and observances of the law instead of the freedom people can have in Christ? Why was he always warning churches against the Judaizers instead of telling churches to listen to them? Because "by the deeds of the law no flesh will be justified in His sight" (Romans 3:20). There is nothing in the law that can make people righteous— not circumcision, not dietary restrictions, not keeping feast days or traditions, or anything else.

Paul said in Romans 10:12, "There is no distinction between Jew and Greek, for the same Lord over all is rich to all who call upon Him." And in verse 13 he adds, "Whoever calls on the name of the LORD shall be saved." Calling on the name of the Lord is how Jews are saved, not by keeping the law.

The only two covenants in the Bible are the Old and New (the word *testament* means "covenant"). Both are blood covenants, and the new covenant is one of "better blood," according to Hebrews 9:11-28. Hebrews 10:4 also tells us "it is not possible that the blood of bulls and goats could take away sins," and yet the animal sacrifices were mandated by the law. Because blood sacrifices were part of the law, and because those sacrifices were insufficient for taking away sin, how can anyone be saved by keeping the law and offering sacrifices of a covenant that has now been fulfilled by Christ?

Dual Covenant Theology is a dangerous doctrine that is simply not true, and we could even say it is a form of antisemitism because it keeps God's chosen people from coming to the only One who can save them—Yeshua, Jesus.

9. Will Israel play a role in the destruction of Damascus prophesied in Isaiah 17:1?

Amir: I believe that the destruction of Damascus which is in Syria—will be the match that lights the fuse that will ignite the war described in Ezekiel chapters 38–39. And there is a very good chance that we will see this happen, but then be raptured before the Ezekiel war begins. Scripture doesn't tell us the exact timing, so we cannot know for sure, but of all the events that are still in line to take place as we approach the end times, I think there is a good chance we might see the destruction of Damascus.

Remember, Syria is not mentioned in the Ezekiel 38–39 war. This does not necessarily mean that Syria will not exist anymore, but it may indicate that Syria will lose its status as a sovereign country. It is possible that Syria will have to be completely devastated for that nation to not be part of the enemy forces that come against Israel from the north, as prophesied in Ezekiel 38.

There are two other things that will likely take place in connection with the Ezekiel war. First, because we do not see anyone come to Israel's aid, it's possible that the United States, which has long been an ally of Israel, will have declined to the point of being unable to respond. And second, when the enemy forces are defeated, it could open the door for the rise of the antichrist from the new version of the old Roman Empire. I believe that the peace that the antichrist will offer to Israel is a peace that the world will desire after the Ezekiel war is over.

Though we don't know exactly when we will be raptured, we do know it will be before the antichrist rises to introduce his false peace. That's because 2 Thessalonians 2:7-8 tells us that "the lawless one will be revealed" *after* the one "who now restrains…is taken out of the way." The restrainer is the Holy Spirit, who dwells in all believers. When we are raptured, the restrainer will be removed. Not until then will the lawless one—or the antichrist—become known.

Barry: It seems logical to conclude that the destruction of Damascus will be a catalyst for other prophetic events. Damascus is about 45 miles north of the border of Israel, and lately, Israel has been striking Iranian military targets in Syria that pose a danger to Israel. Because Syria is to the north, and because Ezekiel 38 tells us that the coalition of nations that will invade Israel will come from the north, it seems the destruction of Damascus could be the catalyst that sparks the war.

Ezekiel 38:10-13 tells us there will be economic reasons behind the invasion against Israel. But an Israeli strike on Damascus might cause the international community to think that an attack against Israel is justified, and this may be why there will be virtual silence from world leaders when the invasion occurs. Ezekiel 38:13 seems to indicate it will be the Arab Gulf States who question the invasion. But the rest of the world will probably remain silent because they see the destruction of Damascus as justification for a massive attack against Israel.

Another prophetic event that could happen after the Ezekiel war is the building of the third temple on the Temple Mount. Ezekiel says that the invading armies will experience all kinds of destruction: an earthquake, flooding rain, and great hailstones of fire (Ezekiel 38:19-22). We read that God will make it very clear that He Himself comes to Israel's defense (verse 23). After that, who is going to protest against Israel building the third temple? Radical Islam will have been destroyed, God will have made it clear whose side He is on, and the antichrist will likely exploit this to his own advantage and offer to bring peace to the Middle East.

Because the antichrist cannot rise to power until the church is taken out of the way, if it turns out that the Ezckiel war begins before the tribulation and ends during the tribulation, we should be looking for the glorious appearing of our great God and Savior Jesus Christ at any moment! After all, Syria is in the news every day now, and the Russian, Iranian, and Turkish armies who will lead the invasion with Sudan and Libya in tow have already established a presence in Syria.

10. Do you think we'll get to see the building of the third temple?

Barry: No, but we do know a temple will be built at the spot where the previous temples were located. We know that the beast who is described in Revelation 13—that is, the antichrist—will take away the daily sacrifices at the temple, according to Daniel 11:31. For there to be sacrifices means a temple must be in place so the antichrist can stop the sacrifices.

Also, in Matthew 24:15, Jesus warned about an act called the abomination of desolation. This was also described by the prophet Daniel, who said this abomination would occur at the midpoint of the tribulation (Daniel 9:27). So Jesus Himself made a connection between the third temple and the antichrist. Based on this information, we can conclude that the temple will be built during the first part of the tribulation. Because all Christians will be taken up at the rapture, none of us will be here to see the temple being rebuilt.

As Amir pointed out earlier, the apostle Paul said in 2 Thessalonians

2:7-8 that the lawless one—the beast who commits the abomination of desolation—cannot be revealed until the hindering force of the Holy Spirit within the church is taken out of the way. Not until after that can the lawless one be revealed. For this reason, we will not see the third temple being built.

Amir: Because it is the antichrist who will offer a peace treaty to Israel, it is also the antichrist who will allow the Jews to build a temple. We know that we will not be here to see the antichrist, which means we won't see the building of the third temple. We won't be here during that time of deception, or the hour of trial, which Jesus will take us *out* of, not *through* (Revelation 3:10).

This is why I don't understand why people debate about the location of the third temple. The Jews themselves have already determined that it's going to be where the Dome of the Rock is. They have already prepared the blueprints for the third temple, and they have already made the trumpets, bowls, priestly garments, and other implements needed for temple worship and sacrifice. All these things are in place and ready for use. All that remains is for the temple itself to be built. Why would we question how the temple can possibly be built when the Bible says it will happen? And when so many people in Israel are getting ready for it? Bible prophecy tells us the temple will be rebuilt on the Temple Mount, but we won't be here to see it happen.

We also need to remember that the third temple will not be sanctioned by God. It will exist, but it will not be the temple of the Messiah; it will be the temple of the antichrist. For this reason, Christians should not be sending their money to support the building of the third temple. Let the devil build his own temple; the church shouldn't be financing it. Scripture tells us there will be a fourth temple when Christ sets up His millennial kingdom on earth. And He will rule the world from His throne in Jerusalem. That is the temple we should look forward to.

CHAPTER 2

THE
CHURCH

THE CHURCH

Just before Jesus ascended to heaven, He told the disciples, "You shall receive power when the Holy Spirit has come upon you; and you shall be witnesses to Me in Jerusalem, and in all Judea and Samaria, and to the end of the earth" (Acts 1:8). In the same way that Israel was meant to be God's witness to the world, He then passed this role on to the church. It is now from the church that the world hears about the truth of salvation through Jesus Christ, and it is from the church that the second collection of writings, the New Testament, was added to God's Word.

Prior to His ascension, Jesus gave the disciples—and all believers through the ages—a mandate. We are to serve as witnesses of God to the ends of the earth. This charge is clearly stated in Matthew's account of the Great Commission, where Jesus said, "Go therefore and make disciples of all the nations, baptizing them in the name of the Father and of the Son and of the Holy Spirit, teaching them to observe all things that I have commanded you; and lo, I am with you always, even to the end of the age" (Matthew 28:19-20).

This is where our challenge comes in. We are to serve as instruments in God's hand to make Him known and to proclaim the gospel message. Paul asked the question, "If the trumpet makes an uncertain sound, who will prepare for battle?" (1 Corinthians 14:8). What kind of sound are you making on behalf of our Lord? When your neighbor or coworker or family member speaks with you, are they hearing the song of the Lord or just worldly noise?

We are to alert the lost about who God is and what is about to happen—that judgment is coming. The only way we can make sure that our sound is loud and our notes are true is to be daily in the Word of God and in prayer. This will allow the Spirit of God to fill our minds and His breath to fill our lungs, so that we will speak and display God's truth in all we say and do.

As we approach the end times, we are also approaching the end of the church age. Soon, our Lord will rapture us and take us to be with Him in heaven. So we must carry out our Lord's work with a sense of urgency, before our opportunities to do so run out.[3]

1. Is the falling away described in 2 Thessalonians 2:3 a departure from the faith or the rapture of the church?

Amir: There are legitimate differences of opinion on this question, and this isn't an issue we should allow ourselves to be divided over. Also, our interpretation of this passage does not affect the status of our salvation.

I am convinced that the writer, the apostle Paul, used the Greek word *apostasía* because he was specifically inspired to use that term.

He could have used other words if he wanted to say something other than what *apostasía* means, which is "to depart from truth." But Paul was inspired to use *apostasía* because that is the word God wanted him to use.

For us to better understand how to interpret *apostasía*, we can go to the one other place in the New Testament where it is used: Acts 21:21. There, Paul is accused (*apostasía*) of forsaking Moses' law. Some people, in their attempt to explain 2 Thessalonians 2:3, go to other words or verbs that are derived from *apostasía*, but it's not always helpful to look at other words to interpret a specific word that was used in a specific context. The only context in which *apostasía* is used in the New Testament means "to depart from the truth or from the Word," not to depart from the world.

Personally, I believe there are enough evidences in God's Word that talk about the pre-tribulation rapture that *apostasía* is not needed to make the case for it. Whatever your position may be on how to best understand what *apostasía* means, the most important thing to know is that you must be born again in order to be saved. We can debate this respectfully until the time that we are called home, and at that time, we'll find out whose interpretation was correct. But by then, none of us will care, for we will be with Jesus.

Barry: I agree with what Amir said about the need for us to not be divided by differences like this one. We are the body of Christ, and we are to be known by our love for one another, not our disagreements. We need to love one another and show the world that we have the love of Christ in us by displaying love to each other even when we debate issues like this one—issues that have nothing to do with the essentials of the faith or salvation.

Let's look first at the language in the opening statement of 2 Thessalonians 2, where Paul mentions the *parousia*, the second coming of Christ. He tells the church this hasn't happened yet because there's going to be a "gathering together" first, or the *episynagoge*. That's the same Greek term used in Hebrews 10:25 to refer to the church assembly. It means "to assemble together the complete collection." The "gathering" in 2 Thessalonians 2:1 is talking about the rapture of the church.

To build on what Amir said about letting Scripture interpret Scripture, the word *apostasía* appears in the Greek translation of the Old Testament, the Septuagint. In Joshua 22:22, it is translated as "rebellion," and in Jeremiah 2:19, it is translated as "backslidings." So again, all the biblical contexts of *apostasía* are in reference to defecting or departing from the truth. This is also in line with what Paul wrote in 2 Timothy 4:3 about a time coming when people will not endure sound doctrine but will prefer fables over facts. One of the greatest proofs of the meaning of *apostasía* is that we are watching this happen right before our eyes!

Also, when it comes to interpreting Scripture, we need to be careful about establishing word meanings from ancient secular writings. This Greek book or that Greek text may have used *apostasia* to speak of a change of location or departure from once place to another, but that has nothing to do with how the word is used in the Bible. Context is everything, and secular writings do not establish context for sacred truth.

Again, this is an issue on which we can agree to disagree and not condemn each other because this is not a salvation-related matter.

2. Are Critical Race Theory and the social justice movement making their way into the church prophetic?

Barry: Without question, yes. In the introductory statements of the Olivet Discourse, Jesus made it clear that there will be strife prior to His return. He said that "nation will rise against nation, and kingdom against kingdom" (Matthew 24:7). This is not a redundant statement; there are two different Greek words used in those seemingly parallel phrases.

A "kingdom" speaks of a governmental system, so countries are going to be at odds with one another. The word "nation," however, is *ethnos* in the Greek text, from which we get the English word *ethnic*. Jesus was saying there are going to be ethnic tensions in the last days that are spurred on by demonic forces that are driving things in the direction of all things anti-God and anti-Israel. The word *ethnos* could be understood as referring to non-Jewish people. When used in the Septuagint, *ethnos* speaks of foreign nations that do not worship the true God. This implies that people bound by religious or ideological ties will also be at odds with each other, in addition to the racial tensions that will be on the rise as the day of the Lord approaches.

The saddest part about Critical Race Theory and issues like white privilege making their way into the church is that they deny what Ephesians 2:14-16 tells us about the church being "one new man" in Christ. These views overlook the fact that, in the body of Christ, there are no racial or gender distinctions. Rather, we are a single people known as the church. As Galatians 3:28 says, "There is neither Jew nor Greek, there is neither slave nor free, there is neither male nor female; for you are all one in Christ Jesus." There is no room for racism or favoritism in the body of Christ; we are all to be of one mind and heart.

Also, Jesus said in John 13:35 that the world will know we are His disciples by the love we show to one another. The church is one body made up of people from every tribe, tongue, nation, and people from every walk of life. The church is not here to right the wrongs of the world, but to rescue people's souls from death.

Amir: Yes, Critical Race Theory and social justice are pushing the world, and much of the church, in a direction where the ethnic tensions are ultimately going to become the whole world against Israel, as Zechariah 12:3 says. We already see this happening in the church through Replacement Theology, which teaches that the church has replaced Israel in God's plan. We are also seeing this in those churches that participate in the Boycott, Divestment, Sanctions (BDS) movement, which is anti-Israel.

As Barry said, ideologically driven aggressions are going to increase in frequency and become worse in the days before the rapture. Like labor pains, these hostilities will become more intense as we draw closer to meeting the Lord in the air.

We see this happening all around us. International support of Israel is changing. More and more world leaders who claim to be against antisemitism also happen to be against Israel. They deny Israel's right to all its land, and the loudest of these opponents share the same religious ideology as the adherents of Islam.

Nations are at war all over the world even though in many cases, we are talking about a war of words. Ethnic tensions are rising because of the social justice movement, and people are being blamed for injustices in the world merely because of the color of their skin, much like Jewish people have long been blamed for many tensions and problems simply because they are Jewish.

All these things fit well with what Paul wrote in 2 Timothy 3 about perilous times in the last days. The first problem he mentions is that people will be lovers of self (verse 2), and he goes on to say they will be traitors (verse 4). This is what we see happening today, which tells us the end is at hand and our redemption is drawing near.

3. What does the parable of the ten virgins signify?

Amir: I believe this parable shows the difference between faith and religion. There are many people who claim to be Christians simply because they were born in a nation that has many Christians, or they were born to parents who profess to be Christians, or because their birth certificate says they are "Christian." But that doesn't mean a person knows Jesus as Savior and Lord. In Matthew 7:21-23, Jesus said there is coming a day when many people will say, "Lord, Lord, have we not prophesied in your name, cast out demons in your name, and done many wonders in your name?" And Jesus will respond, "I never knew you; depart from Me, you who practice lawlessness!"

This makes me think of those mafia movies in which mobsters do all kinds of horrible things and yet they still go to church on Sunday. Even in Israel, you will see Jewish criminals show up in court with a yarmulke and act pious because they think appealing to religion is somehow going to help them.

But to be religious is not the same as being a true believer and walking in the Spirit. If there is one thing Jesus was very clear about in His ministry, it's that religion is not the answer. When Jesus said that following the law is not enough for a person to be saved, that's when people wanted to kill Him.

Today, there are people who get upset when you tell them it's not enough to go to church, to confess to a priest, or to put money in the offering. When you say that no amount of good works can save a person, these people get angry. In the parable of the wise and foolish virgins in Matthew 25:1-13, the virgins without oil were the religious and the virgins with oil were the righteous. The righteous were invited to the wedding feast, and the unprepared could not go. They missed the wedding because they were not ready.

Barry: It's important to keep in mind that in Scripture, the Holy Spirit is symbolically represented by oil. In Exodus 35, when Moses was given the very specific instructions for how to build the tabernacle, he was told that oil was for the light (verses 8, 14, 28). Because we as Christians are the light of the world (Matthew 5:14), we need the Holy Spirit flowing in and through us so we can be that light.

There's been a considerable amount of unnecessary confusion about the parable of the ten virgins. Some have said it implies a partial filling of the Spirit, which is not true. Others say it pictures those who are Christians but are not ready for the rapture, which also is not true. Knowing Jesus as your Savior is what makes you ready and makes you the light of the world, as symbolized by the Holy Spirit.

I agree with Amir's point that the foolish virgins represent people who think they're ready for the rapture but are not. They assume they're ready for the wedding, but they aren't because their lamps are empty or half-full with rituals. They have religion but not the Holy Spirit, and if they don't have the Spirit, it's because they haven't been born again. The word picture Jesus painted in this parable was one of being ready versus being religious.

The lesson? Don't be searching the world for what can only come through a relationship with Christ. We need to be born not of water, but of the Spirit. Notice that the foolish virgins requested oil for their lamps, which were about to go out. The wise virgins gave a wise answer—they said, "We can't do that; you need to have your own oil." There is no proxy salvation. Each person must receive Christ on their own so they can be ready for the wedding when the time comes.

This passage is not teaching a partial rapture, nor is it implying that you can be saved but not filled with the Spirit. The point is not that they were all virgins, but that five were wise and five were foolish. Five were ready, and five weren't.

4. What about those who claim they are having prophetic dreams and visions—should we listen to them? Are such dreams and visions valid?

Barry: It's important to recognize that dreams and visions are a part of the last-days scenario. They haven't come to an end, nor have any of the gifts of the Spirit. Jesus said in Matthew 11:13 that the prophets prophesied until John, meaning John was the last of the prophets in the Old Testament sense. Here, we're talking about prophets as those who spoke about the future and revealed the will of God.

Hebrews 1:1-2 tells us that in times past, God spoke to the fathers "by the prophets." But in these last days, He has "spoken to us by His Son." So when people have a vision or a dream, it is because the Lord wants to communicate something to them—maybe for their protection, or to give a revelation or personal encouragement. But it would not be a revelation for the whole church as were the messages that the prophets spoke to Israel.

We must also remember that because the canon of Scripture is closed, the Bible is complete. Second Peter 1:3 says that "His divine power has given to us all things that pertain to life and godliness," including the entire history of humanity from beginning to end and many specific details along the way. Everything we need is in God's Word. Therefore, we must be careful and even wary when someone says they have a word from the Lord for the whole church with regard to current events or the future. Scripture has already given us the information God intends for us to have.

Though we do not know every detail of what will happen in the future, God has given us enough to know the season of His return. He specifically urges us "to stir up love and good works, not forsaking the assembling of ourselves together, as is the manner of some, but exhorting one another, and so much the more as you see the Day approaching" (Hebrews 10:24-25).

Amir: We've been hearing about how God is giving dreams and visions to people who live in Iran and other countries in the Middle

East. Many people are coming to know Him through these means because it is not possible to reach very many people in these countries with missionaries and the gospel.

Revelation 14:6 tells us that during the tribulation, an angel will preach the everlasting gospel to people of every nation, tribe, and tongue while flying over the earth. And the prophet Joel wrote about a future time when prophecies, visions, and dreams would be experienced by young people and old in Israel (Joel 2:28-29).

We know from Zechariah 12:10 that the Jews who survive to the end of the tribulation are going to recognize Jesus as their Savior and mourn for the One who was pierced by their fathers. We don't want to limit or quench the Spirit, but we are told in 1 John 4:1, "Do not believe every spirit, but test the spirits." Any dream or vision that points away from Jesus or contradicts the Bible is not of God. That's how we are to test all dreams and visions—do they line up with Scripture?

We live in a time when people are hungry for an experience with the supernatural. And there are many people today who claim no association with any organized religion yet describe themselves as being "spiritual." Some of them end up seeking a connection with the spiritual realm and, sadly, with the enemy, who loves to masquerade as an angel of light (2 Corinthians 11:14).

Tarot cards and mediums, psychics and spiritualists are all the rage in these days. We must be careful in these last days because Satan, who "walks about like a roaring lion" (1 Peter 5:8), loves to say things that sound good but aren't true. Satan does this in the spiritual realm, which would include the domain of dreams and visions.

If what you read or hear conflicts with God's Word, it is not from God. If it adds to God's Word, it is not from God. If it denies or takes away from God's Word, it's not from God. This is how we test the spirits, including the spiritual experiences of dreams and visions.

5. Can a demon possess a Christian? And if so, will this happen more and more in the last days?

Amir: If you have the Holy Spirit in you, it's the Spirit who possesses you, and Satan cannot displace the Spirit. However, that doesn't mean you're shielded from demonic activity or the possibility of any demonic presence around you. Demonic activity can take place in your midst.

I know Christians who suffer from bad dreams, panic attacks, and anxiety, but that doesn't mean they have demons in them. However, it *is* possible that they are struggling with the demonic realm around them. After all, the Bible clearly states in Ephesians 6:12-13 that "we do not wrestle against flesh and blood, but against principalities, against powers, against the rulers of the darkness of this age, against the spiritual hosts of wickedness." And where are they? "In the heavenly places." So it makes sense that there is some kind of demonic presence around us.

But when you have the Holy Spirit in you, and when you are in the Word of God, and you have a spiritually healthy life with support from fellow believers, your ability to withstand the enemy is much greater. It's like having a spiritual immune system: The more time you spend with God, the less the enemy can do to you. But the more you allow the world in your life, the more the world can affect you.

As far as seeing more spiritual darkness as we approach the last days, yes, we can expect that. Revelation 12:12 says that when Satan realizes he has a short time left, he will express great wrath. So there will be an increase in demonic activity and harassment as we get closer to the end.

Barry: We must first recognize the difference between possession and oppression. It's entirely possible for a Christian to be oppressed by the adversary; that's why we're told to take our thoughts captive against "every high thing that exalts itself against the knowledge of God" (2 Corinthians 10:5). The devil never gives up; he comes only "to steal, and to kill, and to destroy" (John 10:10).

Satan will target our hope and joy because He can't snatch us from the Father's grasp nor separate us from His love (John 10:28-29; Romans 8:35-39). But there's nothing he likes more than a grumpy, downtrodden, joyless Christian.

Yes, we will face circumstances in life that are discouraging, painful, and hard. And we may find ourselves downcast or depressed. During those times, we need to remember 1 John 4:4, which says, "You are of God, little children." You are His possession. You are His; He is yours. The passage goes on to say, "He who is in you is greater than he who is in the world." Also, when Jesus was accused of casting out demons by the name or the power of Beelzebub, He said that "every city or house divided against itself will not stand" (Matthew 12:25).

While Christians can go through dry or painful times or be demonically harassed, which we see happen repeatedly in the Psalms, it doesn't mean we're possessed. The power of the Holy Spirit within us is greater than the power of the devil's spirits who are after us. So no, a Christian cannot be demon-possessed—not even in the last days. Satan can certainly oppress us, and he will spend a lot of time trying to do that, but we can, by the power of God within us, manifest the weapons of our warfare and fight the good fight of faith.

We also need to remember that Satan knows the Scriptures too.

He quoted them to Jesus during His 40 days of temptation. The devil is watching world events unfold, and Revelation 12:12 says that Satan recognizes that his days are numbered. Because he comes only to steal, kill, and destroy, it stands to reason that the less time he has remaining, the more aggressive he will become in his efforts to rob us of our hope and joy through his oppressive tactics. But greater is He who is in us than he who is in the world!

6. Should the predominantly Gentile church celebrate the Jewish feast days? Is it wrong to do so?

Barry: Let's start by pointing out that there is no such thing as a "Gentile" church. As Paul said in Ephesians 2:14-16, Christ created "one new man" when He began the church. With that said, we need to remember that the seven feasts of Israel were all pointing to someone.

The spring feasts—the Passover, the Feast of Unleavened Bread, the Feast of Firstfruits, and Pentecost—all point to events connected with the first coming of Jesus Christ. Jesus is the Passover lamb, the Feast of Unleavened Bread points to His sinless nature, the Feast of Firstfruits speaks of His conquest of death and becoming the firstborn from the dead (meaning He was the first to arise from the dead and ascend into heaven and is alive forevermore), and Pentecost commemorates God giving His law to Israel was fulfilled in Christ fulfilling the law and giving His church the Holy Spirit.

The Fall Feasts—the Feast of Trumpets, the Day of Atonement or Yom Kippur, and the Feast of Tabernacles—all relate to events surrounding Jesus' second coming. The Feast of Trumpets will be fulfilled by Jesus' return, the Day of Atonement will be fulfilled when the Lord saves all Israel, and the Feast of Tabernacles will be fulfilled by the millennial kingdom. As long as Christians remember what the feasts point to, they are wonderful observances.

Amir: We need to recognize these are the feasts of the Lord. He gave them to Israel because the people were to bring God's Word and commandments to the world. But because the first coming saw Jesus fulfill the first three (Passover, the Feast of Unleavened Bread, the Feast of Firstfruits) and the coming of the Holy Spirit fulfilled the fourth (Pentecost), we can celebrate these feasts with greater joy and satisfaction.

I don't want to tell you that if you don't celebrate these festivals, you're not a good believer. But if the Lord gave us festivals that allow us to celebrate and remember Christ, why not? Christmas and Easter are different because there are many pagan roots to both. However, if the whole world is celebrating Christmas and Easter, we can use them as platforms to show people who Jesus really is—these are opportunities to explain Christ's birth and His resurrection. Note that Jesus went to Jerusalem to celebrate the Festival of Lights, which is not biblical. This was a traditional festival, and even Jesus went to Jerusalem along with other people. Why? Because that was His chance to speak about being the light of the world.

I'll never forget the day I read a specific passage in Isaiah chapter 1. I almost lost my breath when I read these words: "The New Moons, the Sabbaths, and the calling of assemblies—I cannot endure iniquity and the sacred meeting. Your New Moons and your appointed feasts My soul hates; they are a trouble to Me, I am weary of bearing them" (verses 13-14). I asked, "What? You hate the festivals that You told us to celebrate?" Then I realized God was saying, "I hate what you have turned them into. You just automatically observe these because you have to. But you don't even know what these events are all about, and you don't know what they mean."

Then God said through Isaiah, "Wash yourselves, make your-selves clean; put away the evil of your doings from before My eyes... Come now, and let us reason together" (verses 16, 18).

The same applies to us today. When we receive Christ as our Savior, we are made clean and are forgiven. Now we can come before God and celebrate these holidays "in spirit and truth" (John 4:24). But if you approach these feasts from a religious perspective, you will miss the point behind them. And if you're going to say we need to observe these feasts and merely focus on the traditions that go with them, then you're going to miss what the feasts point to: Jesus.

7. What is Kingdom Now theology? Is it biblical?

Amir: The Bible clearly states in John 14:1-3 that Jesus has gone to prepare a place for us so we can be where He is. Scripture never says we are to prepare a place for Him so He can come to us. The New Apostolic Reformation movement teaches the unbiblical view that the church has to get the world ready for the return of Jesus and that He cannot come back until they do.

In Matthew 24:44, Jesus said that He is coming at a time when He is not expected. If the church is supposed to make the world ready, then we would know when to be ready for Him. Jesus also warned that things will not be improving when He comes, but rather, they will be morally and spiritually declining. Things will be as bad as they were in the days of Noah.

To say that the church must establish God's kingdom on earth before Jesus can come and rule puts the church in control of the second coming. It also means there is no rapture, and if that is true, what about the seventieth week of Daniel? When is the tribulation? What do Zechariah 14 and Revelation 19 mean when Jesus comes and fights against His enemies and those who gather against Jerusalem? Who will He be fighting against?

Kingdom Now theology is not biblical; it is antibiblical. It is the opposite of what the Bible actually teaches about the world when Jesus comes back.

Barry: The proponents of Kingdom Now theology are called the "new apostles," and what they teach goes against the myriad of details the Bible has given us about the last days. Scripture talks about how a coalition of nations will invade Israel, how there will be many people in the church who will defect from the truth, and how the last days will be perilous and as evil as the days of Noah. We are told that lawlessness will abound and that the love of many will grow cold, and that we, God's people, will be hated for His name's sake. We are also told that antisemitism will spread globally. What we are *not* told is that there will be a new set of apostles who are equal in power and authority to those who were originally appointed by Jesus. This in and of itself disqualifies the movement.

We also need to note that Kingdom or Dominion Theology teaches what is called the Seven Mountain Mandate. This mandate states that the church must have dominion over the seven seats of power in the world, which are said to be education, religion, the family, business, the government/military, the arts/entertainment, and the media. If the church must have dominion over these seven areas before Jesus can return, He's not coming anytime soon. The Bible says there will be one religion before Jesus comes back, and it will be Satan worship (worship of the beast). The Bible says that the antichrist—and not the church—will control global commerce during the tribulation. And he—not the church—will have authority over the military.

For these many reasons, and because God's Word does not say

anything about a second group of apostles coming during the last days to usher in the kingdom, we can conclude that Dominion Theology and the New Apostolic Reformation are apostate. Our world is not getting better. The Bible makes it clear Jesus will return when things can't get any worse.

8. Will the church go through any of the tribulation?

Barry: No, the tribulation is a time of God's wrath, and 1 Thessalonians 5:9 tells us that "God did not appoint us to wrath." Many people wonder if what Jesus said in John 16:33 about having tribulation in this life means the church will go through the tribulation. The Greek word translated "tribulation" means "pressures" or "anguish," and it can also mean "afflictions." But experiencing tribulations and entering into the global time of God's wrath are two different things.

We also need to keep in mind that the tribulation and the seventieth week of Daniel are one and the same. Daniel 9:24 says that 70 weeks are "determined," which means "to decree" or "mark out," for Daniel's people and holy city. The purposes of the tribulation are to complete the discipline of Israel and judge a Christ-rejecting, Satan-serving world. These purposes require the absence of the church because during the seventieth week of Daniel, the antichrist will "prevail against" the saints, and in Matthew 16:18, Jesus said the gates of Hades will not prevail against the church. The saints of the tribulation era cannot be the church, for the church will not go through any of the tribulation.

Amir: In Daniel 8:19, the angel Gabriel explained to Daniel about "the latter time of the indignation," and said that it will occur at the time of the end. "Indignation" is the Hebrew word *zaʾam*, and it means "anger" or "wrath." That tells us that the tribulation, though it is divided into two parts, is all a time of God's wrath. Because the church is not appointed to wrath, the church cannot be present for any of the tribulation. There are some people who believe the rapture to be a pre-wrath event, and because God's wrath will be poured out during the entire tribulation, they actually unknowingly hold to the pre-tribulation rapture position.

We also know from Revelation 3:10 that the Lord has promised the church will be kept *from*, not kept *through*, the hour of testing that is coming upon the whole world. We do not know if there is a gap of time between the rapture and the beginning of the tribulation, but it makes sense for there to be a gap because it will take some time for the world to reorganize itself after such a traumatic event. What we do know for sure is that when the first of the seven seals on the scroll is opened by the One on the throne, the antichrist will ride onto the world scene with a covenant plan to bring peace to the world. This will include bringing an end to the Middle East conflict by making a covenant with the Jews.

When the second seal is opened, the pseudo peace brought by the antichrist will be broken and the world will enter a time of horrible violence. That will be followed by a global famine, after which death by the sword and hunger will kill one-fourth of the earth's population. Because God's wrath will start pouring out with the opening of the seal judgments at the beginning of the tribulation, and because the church will be kept from the hour of testing, there is no reason for the church to be present on earth. Remember, the lawless one who rides the white horse when the first seal is broken cannot be revealed until "He who now restrains" the lawless one's rise to power is taken out of the way (2 Thessalonians 2:7). "He who now restrains" is the Holy Spirit, and Christians are temples of the

Holy Spirit (1 Corinthians 6:19), so again, the church has to be raptured before the man of sin can be revealed.

9. Is the Olivet Discourse only about Israel, or does any of it pertain to the church?

Barry: I believe the Olivet Discourse in Matthew 24–25 (also recorded in Mark 13 and Luke 21) is written to both. Mark's Gospel tells us that this was a private conversation between Jesus and Peter, Peter's brother Andrew, and the sons of thunder, James and John. This discourse was Jesus' answer to their questions about when the destruction of the temple would take place and what would be the signs of His coming and of the end of the age. Jesus never answered the first question—when would there not be one stone "left here upon another" of the Temple and its buildings—but He did answer about the signs of His coming and the end of the age. The four men with Jesus are a bit unique in that they, at the moment of this conversation, were all Jews under the law, yet before any of them died, they were all members of the church, in which there is neither Jew nor Greek, slave nor free, male nor female, as we all make up the body of Christ (Galatians 3:28). So Jesus was talking to four Jews who would soon become four members of the church. The answer is yes, there is application in the Olivet Discourse for both.

The content also bears out that Jesus was talking about the church and Israel, as seen in His use of the phrase "the days before the flood" (Matthew 24:38). The flood was God's wrath poured out on the entire world, and the tribulation will be God's wrath poured out on the entire world. That means the days before the flood parallel the days before God's wrath on the world in the form of the seventieth week of Daniel. We also need to remember that Noah was a Gentile, and these days before the tribulation are "the times of the Gentiles" (Luke 21:24). Jesus said that people will react with indifference to the clear signs of impending judgment—they will be buying and selling, marrying and giving in marriage. Revelation 18 says that during the tribulation, global commerce will cease and the voices of the bridegroom and bride will not be heard anymore. This means Jesus must be referring to before the tribulation, and not before the second coming.

Amir: As Barry said, the Olivet Discourse is a teaching that Jesus gave to the four Jewish disciples who would later become a part of the church. But I believe there is also a third group that is being addressed in the Olivet Discourse, and that is the world. Jesus was speaking to the Jews, the church, and the unbelieving world.

When Jesus used the term "you" in His message, He was not necessarily speaking to "them" as first-century believers, but to "them" in answer to what is going to happen in the future to the Jews, to the church, and to the world. For example, when God said to the people of Israel in Deuteronomy, "You are chosen people," He wasn't referring to the nation of Israel only at that time or to that specific generation. The term "you" obviously speaks to those who will be alive in the future. That's why we can say that Matthew 24 and 25 is a direct answer from Jesus to the questions that relate to Israel, the church, and the world, and not just those He was addressing that day.

Of course, when we teach on the Olivet Discourse, we can see why it is easy to be mistaken and to assume that what Jesus said was only for Israel. Yet Jesus was speaking about the future, and the language He used makes it clear He was speaking to Israel, the church, and the world. That's why it's so important for us to pay careful attention to the context and the words and descriptions.

10. Do our loved ones who have died in Christ have the ability to look down from heaven and see what's happening on earth?

Amir: I always say that in areas where the Bible is silent, we should be silent. Also, when Jesus comes back to the earth to rule and reign for 1,000 years, we will be with Him. We will return in our glorified bodies and see what is happening on the earth at that time. Before that, we will be at the marriage supper of the Lamb, and we will also stand before the judgment seat of Christ to receive our rewards for what we did on earth for His glory. The Bible doesn't say whether we will be able to see what is happening on earth while we are in heaven, but it does say we're going to be very busy in heaven during the seven-year tribulation on earth.

Barry: As Amir said, we are given very limited information about what happens when someone is absent from the body other than the fact they are present with the Lord (2 Corinthians 5:8). We also know they will experience the marriage supper of the Lamb and stand before the judgment seat of Christ. I tend to think that those in heaven will be more focused on where they are than where they were.

Think about all that they will be seeing and experiencing: Four living creatures ceasing not day or night from declaring "Holy, holy, holy, Lord God Almighty, who was and is and is to come!" (Revelation 4:8). Twenty-four elders seated around the throne of God, which is surrounded by a circular emerald-colored rainbow, and before the throne will be a sea of crystal-clear glass (verses 3-6). I have to say I don't think they're going to be wondering what their family members or friends on earth are doing. What we do know is that they are going to be seeing and hearing things that are far beyond anything our finite minds could even imagine.

So, we can only speculate as to what the departed will know about life on earth while they are in heaven with the Lord. It is just that: speculation.

11. Are there any signs related to the church that tell us the rapture is near?

Barry: This question opens the door for so many important things that are vital for us to know, including the fact that 1 Corinthians 2:14 tells us the natural, unregenerate person cannot know the things of God because they are spiritually discerned. In other words, those who are in the church—those who are born-again, Spirit-filled believers—have a supernatural, Spirit-given ability to understand the things of God, including matters relating to eschatology (the study of the last days).

As for the signs that tell us the rapture is near, yes, they are evident, and these signs are for the church alone because the church is the only group of people who will be raptured. Also the fact that we are able to tell the rapture is drawing near does not infringe on the fact that no one knows the day or the hour of Jesus' coming.

In 2 Timothy 3, Paul wrote that "in the last days perilous times will come" (verse 1). He then described what those times will be like, saying that "men will be lovers of themselves, lovers of money, boasters, proud, blasphemers, disobedient to parents, unthankful, unholy, unloving, unforgiving, slanderers, without self-control, brutal, despisers of good, traitors, headstrong, haughty, lovers of pleasure rather than lovers of God, having a form of godliness but denying its power" (verses 2-5).

Then in the next chapter, Paul wrote that "the time will come when they will not endure sound doctrine" (2 Timothy 4:3). That is, people will reject sound doctrines taught by the church. And in 1 John 2, John wrote that because of the increase of people who are "against Christ" and His teachings, we will know "it is the last hour" (verse 18).

For me, one of the greatest indicators of the church's position in the prophetic timeline is found in the letters to the seven churches in Revelation chapters 2 and 3. Before I say why, I need to mention Daniel 12:4, where Daniel was told that the visions he received were about and for a future generation who lived at "the time of the end." This is true of all prophecies related to the last days. Generations of people throughout church history lived without the ability to fully understand the prophecies relating to the rebirth of the nation of Israel and the Ezekiel 38 war. But in recent generations, we have seen Israel be reborn, and today, we see the nations listed in Ezekiel 38:2-6 building alliances with one another, which enables us to understand the passage in ways that previous generations could not.

I believe the same is true of the letters to the seven churches of Asia Minor. At the time they were written, they were sent to seven literal churches in seven literal cities. But Revelation 1:3 describes the entire book as "prophecy," and does not exempt chapters 2 and 3. There are some who believe chapters 2 and 3 are not prophetic in any way, but I believe that in our day, we, much like Daniel was told, can see a chronology of church history contained in the letters that earlier generations could not see.

That means the things we see described in the last letter—the one to the church at Laodicea—represent what will happen during the last portion of church history. John wrote that letter to "the church *of* the Laodiceans," whereas most of the letters were written to churches "in" a city, with the exception of Ephesus, which was written to the church "of" Ephesus. The word "Laodicea" is telling, for it means "the rule of the people." This is a compound Greek word, and *laos* means "people," and *dikao* means "justice" or "rule." The *s* on the end of "Laodiceans" indicates the church has been taken over by the rule of the people. That is why, in verse 20, we find Jesus on the outside knocking to get in.

The people in the church of the Laodiceans claimed they had everything figured out. In their opinion, they were rich and had need of nothing. They did not know, according to Jesus, that their actual condition was wretched, miserable, poor, blind, and naked. He counseled them to buy gold from Him, meaning that which was of true value. This is consistent with what Paul wrote about those who will not put up with sound doctrine (2 Timothy 4:3), as well as what he wrote in 2 Thessalonians 2:3 about there being a defection from truth before the lawless one can be revealed. This is also consistent with what Jesus said about false Christs being the first sign of His coming for His church (Matthew 24:4-5).

It is my belief that we are in the Laodicean age of church history, with these things in mind: In Scripture, the number 7 is the number of completeness, and there is no eighth letter in Revelation 2–3. That means when the church age arrives at the point that is described in the letter to the church of the Laodiceans—at the end of Revelation 3—we should soon expect to hear what John wrote in Revelation 4:1: "Come up here." That is the rapture.

Amir: In Scripture, most of the descriptions of "the day of the Lord" have to do with a time of terrible trial that is going to come upon the sinners that are here on earth. This "day of the Lord" is a time you definitely want to avoid, which you can do when you accept Christ as your Savior and Lord.

The purpose of the day of the Lord is for God to send judgment upon all unbelievers. The reason we know this day has not started is that the antichrist must first arise on the world stage. It is his presence and his covenant with Israel that marks the beginning of the last week of Daniel, or the seven years of the tribulation (Daniel 9:27).

And that is what the Christians in Thessalonica didn't understand. People told them the seventieth week had already begun. But Paul said not to believe anyone who claimed the day of the Lord had already arrived, even if they said this in Paul's name.

The day of the Lord will be a time unlike any other the world has ever seen. There will be a major falling away or apostasy, as well as the rise of the lawless one. But if you're a believer, you don't have to worry about seeing that day. You will be taken up in the rapture before the antichrist is revealed.

The term "the day of the Lord" is another way to describe the seven-year tribulation.

It's definitely not a 24-hour period, just like a week in Daniel 9 is not seven days. The day of the Lord will occur over a period of seven years. As we read the descriptions given to us by the prophets, we know it is synonymous with the seven-year tribulation. Israel will go through it, but not the church, because we are not destined for the wrath of God. We will be taken out of the way. As the Lord said in Revelation 3:10, He will "keep [us] *from* the hour of trial which shall come upon the whole world."

Hebrews 10:25 also makes it clear that the church will be able to "see the Day approaching." We are told that as we see that day coming, we are to be exhorting one another and not forsaking the assembling of ourselves together. I talk about this in my book *The Day Approaching*. It's a day the Jews cannot see because they're not watching for it. They're still waiting for the Messiah to come and set up His rule.

Think about it: Between Isaiah, Ezekiel, Daniel, Amos,

Zechariah, the Olivet Discourse, 1 and 2 Thessalonians, 2 Timothy, Hebrews, Peter's letters, and Revelation, not to mention all the passages in the Psalms and other books that mention prophecy-related events, we have been given a mountain of information about the day that is approaching!

This is why I speak so strongly against sensationalism, for two main reasons: First, we don't need to resort to sensationalism to get people's attention. We have more than enough information to talk about that is actually biblical, so we don't need any kind of clickbait to get people to listen. Second, sensationalism frequently involves speculation that has little or no biblical foundation or backing.

The rebirth of the nation of Israel began the final march toward the day we now see approaching. The church is the only group of people that can see it coming, and the pre-tribulation rapture view is the only one that fits "the day of the Lord" as a time when God deals with Israel and the Christ-rejecting world, whereas believers will be taken up before that time of wrath. For these reasons, we can assume the rapture is not far off as we see evidence that the day is approaching.

THE RAPTURE

THE RAPTURE

Something happens to the church between chapters 3 and 4 of Revelation. The word "church" occurs 19 times in chapters 1–3, then not again until chapter 22. Where did we go? Quite simply, we will have been taken up to heaven. The word we use to describe this event is *rapture*.

In 1 Thessalonians 4:16-17, the apostle Paul gives the details about what will happen:

> The Lord Himself will descend from heaven with a shout, with the voice of an archangel, and with the trumpet of God. And the dead in Christ will rise first. Then we who are alive and remain shall be caught up together with them in the clouds to meet the Lord in the air. And thus we shall always be with the Lord.

After the dead in Christ have been resurrected to Him, those in the church who are still alive on earth will be "caught up" with our formerly dead brothers and sisters in the Lord, and we will meet our Savior in the clouds. The Greek word translated "caught up" is *harpazo*. When the New Testament was translated into Latin, the word became *rapturo*, which is where we get the word *rapture*.

In this way, Jesus will fulfill His promise to the church to "come again and receive you to Myself; that where I am, there you may be also" (John 14:3). In that moment, as 1 Corinthians 15:51-53 says, we will be changed:

> Behold, I tell you a mystery: We shall not all sleep, but we shall all be changed—in a moment, in the twinkling of an eye, at the last trumpet. For the trumpet will sound, and the dead will be raised incorruptible, and we shall be changed. For this corruptible must put on incorruption, and this mortal must put on immortality.

Aren't you looking forward to that? We are living in lowly bodies that are slowly decaying. We are corruptible, and we are corrupting. But that is okay—it's nothing to get upset about because we've got new, upgraded bodies waiting for us.

In that moment when we are taken to be with our Savior, we will say goodbye to the mortal and shalom to immortality. Our body cells won't decay anymore. Sickness won't bother us anymore. We won't be able to die anymore. And we will be with our Savior—forever.[4]

1. What is the rapture of the church?

Amir: The Bible refers to the rapture as a mystery. When Paul described the rapture in 1 Corinthians 15, he started by saying, "Behold, I tell you a mystery..." (verse 51). Then he wrote about the instant translation of mortal human beings into immortal and incorruptible beings. Paul also wrote in 1 Thessalonians 4 that as the church is taken up in the rapture, the dead in Christ will rise first, and we who remain will be raised up as well, and all of us will meet the Lord in the air. Not only will we be changed into our immortal, incorruptible bodies, but we will change location as well.

It is important to recognize that the rapture is described as a mystery, not a secret. The Bible uses both terms: Secrets are things we don't know that God reveals, and mysteries are things the Bible reveals that need investigation to be understood. A mystery is not something that is hidden like a secret, but rather, something that is transformed from shadow to substance. In the Bible, the greatest example of a mystery is the church. It was no secret that God was going to save the Gentiles, as multiple Old Testament passages stated so (for example, Isaiah 60:3; Jeremiah 16:19; Amos 9:12). What was a mystery, something requiring further investigation, was that from the Jews and Gentiles God was creating "one new man" through His Son, bringing down the wall of separation between Jew and Gentile (Ephesians 2:14-15).

Paul also said in 1 Corinthians 15 that when Christians receive their immortal, incorruptible bodies, they will do so "in the twinkling of an eye" (verse 52). The transformation of our bodies from mortal to immortal and from corruptible to incorruptible to meet the Lord in the air with the dead in Christ is going to happen so quickly that Christians all over the world will simply disappear. This will not be a gradual event; it will be instant. The rapture is the taking of the church to be with the Lord forever and will occur in a split second. And the Bible describes the rapture as "the blessed hope" (Titus 2:13).

Barry: There is another important aspect to consider about the rapture beyond the supernatural action involved and its place as an essential doctrine in the Bible. The rapture of the church is not just important to prophecy, it is also a matter of biblical inerrancy. Some people today argue that the Bible doesn't teach the rapture, and yet if we look at what Jesus told His disciples in John 14:1-3 and compare it to Revelation 19, we can see that the rapture of the church is clearly necessary. Jesus said in John 14 He was going to prepare a place for us so that He might come again and receive us unto Himself so we can be where He is. In Revelation 19, we are told that Jesus returns to the earth with the church to rule and reign in righteousness.

If the church returns from heaven with Jesus at the end of the tribulation, how and when did the church get to heaven in the first place? The phrase "come again" in John 14:3 gives us some help. The Greek terms means "to make an appearance again." In 1 Thessalonians 3:13, Paul mentioned "the coming of our Lord Jesus Christ with all His saints." Here, the Greek term *parousia* is used with regard to the second coming. The Bible says in 1 Thessalonians 4:16-17 that Jesus will appear in the air to meet the dead in Christ and those who are alive and remain. This is the event that will make it possible for the church to already be in heaven and return with Jesus at the end of the tribulation. The rapture is the only possible explanation for how the church will end up in heaven and is thus essential to the inerrancy of Scripture. There are a host of other passages that make the rapture of the church an essential doctrine, but these seem to be definitive.

2. Why don't we find the word rapture in the Bible?

Barry: The simple answer is that we do find the word—just not in our English Bibles. We need to remember that the Bible is the Bible in any language it is accurately translated into. The word *rapturos* comes from the Latin translation of the original Greek New Testament word *harpazo* in 1 Thessalonians 4:17. In our English Bibles, the Greek word *harpazo* is translated "caught up." When 1 Thessalonians 4:17 says, "We shall be caught up [*harpazo*] together with them in the clouds to meet the Lord in the air," that speaks of the rapture.

We also need to note that the argument that the absence of the word *rapture* in our English Bibles is evidence it is not a biblical doctrine is easily nullified by the fact that one of the principal doctrines of Scripture is described by another word also not found in the Bible: *Trinity*. The triune nature of the one true God is clearly taught in Scripture without the use of the word *Trinity*. The rapture of the church is also clearly taught in Scripture, and the fact the word *rapture* is not used in English translations does not invalidate the doctrine.

Amir: I agree. The presence of the word is not the important thing, and the concept is clearly biblical. I would also point out that we do find the word *harpazo*, which, in Latin, is *rapturos*, and is used in several places in the Bible. Acts 8:39 tells us that after Phillip baptized the Ethiopian eunuch, he was "caught...away" (*harpazo*) to a town called Azotus. In John 10:29, Jesus said that whomever the Father has given Him no one is able to "snatch" (*harpazo*) them out of the Father's hand. In Matthew 11:12, Jesus talked about how "the violent" seek to "take" the kingdom of heaven "by force" ("force" being *harpazo*). This assures us that being snatched away by force—or being raptured—is a biblical concept.

3. Which Bible passages tell us about the rapture?

Amir: First Corinthians 15:50-54 and 1 Thessalonians 4:13-18 clearly state that God will resurrect believers who have died and

raise up living believers and give them glorified bodies. In 1 Thessalonians 4:18, Paul says to "comfort one another with these words." It
would not be very comforting to hear that the lawless one will come
to power and kill many, if not all, Christians, or those who somehow manage to survive the cataclysmic events happening around
the world during the tribulation. That alone informs us that there is
a way to escape the tribulation, which is very encouraging news no
matter when a person lived. In Revelation 3:10, Jesus also promised
the church at Philadelphia that because they have persevered, they
will be kept from "the hour of trial which shall come upon the whole
world." This also speaks of the rapture of the church.

Barry: First Thessalonians 5:9 says that we, the church, are not
appointed to God's wrath. Revelation 6:17 tells us that during the
opening of the seven seals, every person—from kings to common-
ers—will try to hide in the rocks and caves of the earth, saying,
"The great day of His wrath has come, and who is able to stand?"
That means that the four horsemen of the apocalypse, including
the first rider on the white horse, who is the antichrist, are all part
of God's wrath, and the church does not have an appointment with
those days. The church must first be removed somehow, and it can't
be through death, for that would conflict with Paul's statement in
1 Corinthians 15:51 that we will not die, but we will be changed.

   I also like to point out that in the Old Testament, we have pictures or typologies of the rapture. Noah was lifted above God's wrath
on the whole world, and Lot's physical location was changed before
God poured out His wrath on Sodom and Gomorrah. These events
set a precedent of God taking protective action on the part of His
people before He pours out His wrath. The same will happen before
His wrath is poured out during the seventieth week of Daniel, or the
tribulation—all of which is a time of God's wrath.

4. What is the purpose of the rapture?

Amir: The rapture of the church will set a series of events into motion. Second Thessalonians 2:7-8 says the rapture will allow for the rise of the antichrist to power, and that cannot happen until the restraining force of the Holy Spirit, as expressed through the church, is taken out of the way. The rapture will transition the world out of the church age and into the tribulation, and it will fulfill the prophecies recorded in 1 Corinthians 15:51-54 and 1 Thessalonians 4:13-18.

Most significantly, the rapture will turn global attention to Israel like never before. Daniel was told that 70 weeks were determined for his people and the holy city, and up till now, only 69 of those weeks of years have been fulfilled. The prophet Zechariah said that Jerusalem would become a burdensome stone to the whole world, which will gather against it (Zechariah 12:3). We are currently in an unusual season of prophetic history because, for the first time ever, national Israel and the church exist simultaneously. The rapture will shift the world's attention and God's attention exclusively to national Israel to finish the final week of the 70 weeks of years foretold to Daniel.

Barry: First Thessalonians 5:9 says that the church is not appointed to God's wrath, but "to obtain salvation through our Lord Jesus Christ." The word translated "salvation" means not only what we typically think of when we hear it—that is, the saving of our souls—but it also means "to deliver." The rapture *delivers* the church from God's wrath. Paul also mentioned in 1 Corinthians 15:51-52 that the rapture will happen at the sounding of the last trumpet. This trumpet has nothing to do with the seven trumpet judgments mentioned in Revelation, but rather, it signals the end of the church age and indicates that the beginning of the seventieth week of Daniel is soon to follow.

This is important because the rapture clearly identifies a necessary transition in God's redemptive plan to the nation of Israel. Jesus said the gates of Hades would not prevail against His church (Matthew 16:18), which tells us that the church would continue down through the ages in spite of the devil's attempts to destroy it. The rapture marks the transition point from the church age back to the weeks that God told Daniel were determined for his people and the holy city. The pause in the fulfillment of Daniel's 70 weeks of years indicates that the time between the sixty-ninth and seventieth weeks is distinct from them, and that something will set the fulfillment of those weeks in motion again. That something is the rapture of the church.

5. Are the rapture and the second coming the same event?

Barry: The two events are distinctly separate in Scripture and, depending on whether there is a span of time between the rapture and beginning of the tribulation, there are at least seven years between the two events. The rapture, as described in 1 Corinthians 15:51-52, 1 Thessalonians 4:16-17, and 2 Thessalonians 2:7, has two main features: (1) the transformation and (2) the transportation of the saints, both living and dead, into the presence of the Lord. First Corinthians 15:51-52 speaks of a transformation from mortal corruptibility to immortal incorruptibility in the twinkling of an eye. First Thessalonians 4:16-17 mentions the dead in Christ and those who are alive and remain meeting the Lord in the air. And 2 Thessalonians 2:7 mentions that the hindering force of the Holy Spirit through the church must be "taken out of the way" before the lawless one (the antichrist) can be revealed.

In contrast, the second coming is a time when the Lord will destroy the lawless one with the brightness of His coming (2 Thessalonians 2:8), when He returns with the glorified saints at the end of the tribulation, as recorded in Revelation 19. The rapture will allow for the rise of the antichrist, and the second coming will bring the destruction of the antichrist, so they cannot be the same event.

The rapture is when Jesus comes for the church and meets the saints in the air, and the second coming is when Jesus comes to earth with the church and rules on the earth for 1,000 years.

Amir: While both 1 Thessalonians 4 and 1 Corinthians 15 mention the rapture and the fact that we will be changed, and in both passages Paul mentions the last trumpet, he makes no connection between that trumpet and any of the trumpet judgments of the tribulation. In fact, in 1 Thessalonians 4, Paul is convinced that the rapture is going to happen during his lifetime. He would also say in the very next chapter, in 1 Thessalonians 5:9, that we do not have an appointment with wrath, which means the church will not be present on earth during the tribulation. The believers in Thessalonica were concerned that their brothers and sisters in Christ were dying and thus would miss the rapture. They asked, "What is happening? We thought that we were not going to die, but that we would all be taken up in the rapture."

Paul said to them, "Don't lose hope. You know that those who die in Christ are not dead; rather, they are asleep." In saying this, Paul didn't mention the tribulation. He didn't say anything about bowl and trumpet and seal judgments, or a time of wrath. Instead, he wrote about the blessed hope that we have (Titus 2:13).

The last trumpet of 1 Corinthians 15:52 has to do with the end of the church age. Remember there's another trumpet, associated with the Feast of Trumpets. All the festivals of Israel were, or will be, fulfilled through Christ. I personally believe that the return of Jesus to earth with the church at the second coming will happen on the Feast of Trumpets. I believe that this is when the Jews who survive the tribulation will receive Him as Lord. Then comes the Day of Atonement, when the Jewish people will repent and mourn and cry out, as Zechariah 12:10 says. After Jesus returns with the church to the earth in all His glory, the final feast of the Jews will be fulfilled, the Feast of Tabernacles, which will occur when Christ establishes the millennial kingdom, during which He will tabernacle with us.

The rapture and the second coming of Jesus are clearly two different events. At the rapture He will come for His church, and at the second coming, He will come for the Jews.

6. Can we know when the rapture will take place?

Amir: Jesus said no one knows the day or the hour except the Father (Matthew 25:13), which truly means no one knows the day or the hour. This has to refer to the rapture because this cannot be said of the second coming. The second coming will happen 1,290 days after the daily sacrifice is taken away and 1,260 days after the abomination of desolation takes place, which marks the middle of the seventieth week of Daniel, as Daniel 12:11 tells us.

While we do not know the day or the hour of the rapture of the church, Paul said in Titus 2:13 that we are to be looking for it. He calls it "the blessed hope and glorious appearing"—not *coming*, but *appearing*—of our great God and Savior, Jesus Christ. Hebrews 9:28 says that He will appear a second time for those who eagerly wait for Him—not for the purpose of dying for our sins, but for the purpose of delivering us from our mortal, corruptible bodies. We cannot know the day or hour, but it is clear that we are to be looking for and eagerly awaiting His appearing in the air.

Barry: I have always found it interesting that the one thing we are told we can't know is the one thing we want to know more than anything else. I want to offer a little calculated speculation as to why the rapture is an unknowable day, outside of the fact that Jesus said it is. Imagine what people would do and how they would live if they knew the day and hour. Human nature being what it is, some would certainly put off coming to Christ and repenting of their sins, waiting until the very last minute, because they know the day and hour of the rapture.

If the day and hour were known, many generations of believers would live without the blessed hope, knowing that only death could deliver them from their mortal and corrupt bodies. However, with the day and hour of the rapture unknown to anyone, *every* generation can and should live in eager and hopeful expectation of when our great God and Savior Jesus Christ will appear in the air to meet us and the dead in Christ. I believe we can go as far to say that the fact we don't know the date of the rapture is a great blessing to the church.

As Amir pointed out, in order for us to be able to watch for the glorious appearing, there would have to be things to look for. Those things are not signs of the rapture per se, but they are signs of what follows the rapture, which include the rise of the man of sin, the world entering the tribulation, and all the things that we see developing right now that can only happen if the rapture has taken place.

What would those things be? A wholesale rejection of truth around the world and a strong spirit of delusion. The decrease of the true Bible-teaching, Christ-exalting church, and the increase of the fables and felt-needs church. We would expect to see the formation of a coalition of nations poised to invade Israel from the north, and the normalization of relationships between Israel and some Arab states. The list goes on and on, but the point is this: We don't know when the rapture will happen, but today is a better candidate than yesterday, and if not today, tomorrow will be even more likely than today!

7. What will happen during the rapture?

Barry: Simply put, Paul said in 1 Corinthians 15:51 that "we shall all be changed." This famed passage about the rapture opens with the statement that flesh and blood—meaning mortal human bodies—cannot inherit the kingdom of God. That is why we will all be changed. We will go from having mortal, corruptible flesh-and-blood bodies to having supernatural, immortal, and incorruptible bodies capable of eternal existence.

The rapture, the snatching away by force, is when this transformation will take place. Paul also used the illustration of the twinkling of an eye to give an indication of how rapidly this will take place. We also know from 1 Thessalonians 4:17 that this change will occur somewhere between the surface of the earth and the meeting point with the Lord in the air. The dead in Christ will be made instantaneously incorruptible and immortal, and those alive at the time will experience the same transformation.

We have all seen artistic portrayals of clothes left behind or empty shoes with a sliver of smoke rising from them to depict this rapid departure. But we are not told much of anything beyond the fact we will be changed instantly into immortal, incorruptible beings.

Amir: In Philippians 3:21, Paul gives us a small glimpse into what we can expect at the rapture when he says that our lowly bodies will be conformed to Christ's glorious body. That means our bodies will be like that of Jesus' after His resurrection. Remember, He could appear in a room without using a door (John 20:19). On the day He rose from the dead, He walked with two dejected disciples on the road to Emmaus, and they did not recognize Him until He allowed them to. After that, He instantly vanished from their sight (Luke 24:13-31).

We will go from having lowly bodies that are growing old and perishing to having glorious bodies. We will finally be freed from the consequences of the fall of man in the garden. We will no longer be subject to death. And we will have minds that are transformed and renewed and able to rule in righteousness with the Lord during the millennium. At the rapture, we'll get a complete makeover in the twinkling of an eye.

8. Who will be raptured?

Amir: Every born-again believer who is alive on earth at the time when the trumpet sounds will be raptured. This is what Paul wrote in 1 Thessalonians 4:16-17: "The Lord Himself will descend from heaven with a shout, with the voice of an archangel, and with the trumpet of God. And the dead in Christ will rise first. Then we who are alive and remain shall be caught up together with them in the clouds to meet the Lord in the air." This is the glorious appearing of our great God and Savior Jesus Christ. He won't come down to the earth; He will meet the whole church in the air. The dead in Christ will be resurrected in glorified bodies, and the alive in Christ will be changed in the twinkling of an eye.

The rapture is for living believers only and is specific to one generation and one moment in time. The dead in Christ are not raptured; rather, they are raised from the dead. Living believers will instantly experience what Paul wrote in Philippians 3:21 about our lowly bodies being conformed to Jesus' glorious body. We will become like Him in the sense of becoming eternal beings.

Barry: What a great privilege it is to be alive in the generation that will not pass away! The fact that we will bypass death—and be supernaturally transformed into the likeness of Jesus, as John said in 1 John 3:2—should lift our hearts and minds above all that the world is experiencing right now. To think that an event Jesus promised on the same night He was betrayed is going to be realized some 2,000 years later when He comes to receive us unto Himself at any time now is beyond wonderful! Every born-again Christian who is alive on earth at the sound of the trumpet will be raptured. My advice is that you make sure you will be among them.

That is why Jesus gave the admonition in Matthew 24:44 to be ready, for He is coming when He is least expected. The fact that we are to live in expectation of His glorious appearing, combined with Jesus' word that He would come at a time when He is least expected, gives us every reason to make sure we're ready. And based on what we see happening around us, the hour is late, the time is at hand, and we should keep looking up, for our redemption is drawing near!

9. What will happen to those who are left behind?

Barry: This is one of those questions that isn't being asked by those who need to be asking it the most. The tribulation will be an unprecedented time of the wrath of God on the earth. The flood was global and killed billions, while eight righteous people were lifted above God's wrath and were spared. Jesus said of this time of divine wrath that no flesh would survive if He didn't return and stop it (Matthew 24:22).

The tribulation will begin when the antichrist establishes a seven-year covenant with Israel. This will be followed by a time of murder and famine that kills one-fourth of the world's population, and remarkably, things will get a lot worse from there. All sea life will be destroyed, all the fresh water of the earth will be made bitter (radioactive, I believe), the grass and trees will be burned up, and an army numbering 200 million horsemen will kill a third of mankind. After that, locusts from the bottomless pit will torment people for five months to the point they seek death but cannot find it.

The sun, likely shooting out an unprecedented solar flare, will scorch people's bodies, and that will be followed by a darkness that is so dark and cold it causes people to gnaw their tongues because of the pain. Then an earthquake of a magnitude that has never occurred before will cause immense destruction. These are just a few of the cataclysmic events Revelation reveals will occur during the tribulation.

Those who dwell on the earth will know they are experiencing the wrath of God. But tragically, rather than repent, they will call on the rocks and mountains, saying, "Fall on us and hide us from the face of Him who sits on the throne and from the wrath of the Lamb!" (Revelation 6:16). Again, this is but a fraction of how terrible this time will be on the earth.

Amir: The tribulation will be a time unlike any the world has ever seen. Not only because of cataclysmic events, but also because of the extent of spiritual deception and delusion. Paul told the church in Thessalonica that those who would not receive the love of the truth will be sent a "strong delusion, that they should believe the lie" (2 Thessalonians 2:10-12). The antichrist will control all the buying and selling that takes place on earth, causing all who want to do business to take a mark on their right hand or forehead. This mark will not just be a pass that allows you to do business, it will also serve as a sign of allegiance to Satan and the antichrist and his lie of claiming to be God.

The antichrist will behead those who do not take the mark, and this will be the fate of those who have the testimony of Jesus, those who are tribulation saints. They are not the church, but are people who will be saved during the tribulation (Revelation 7:14). Immediately after the rapture, there will be a time of chaos and confusion on the earth, and the antichrist will use this to promise he can bring about a solution. Daniel 11:21 says he will take power over the world "by intrigue," which will likely include slippery speech and deceptive promises.

Anyone who is postponing a decision to receive Christ as Savior until after the rapture and during the tribulation should think again. Driverless cars and pilotless planes are not just scenes from a movie about the rapture, they will be a reality in the twinkling of an eye, and the rapture itself will be an event that many who are left behind will not survive. Also, the fear will be so great and the delusion so strong that countless people will fall prey to believing the lie. Don't take a chance and postpone making a commitment to Christ until after the rapture, because you may not even survive it. As 2 Corinthians 6:2 says, "now is the day of salvation."

10. Are there other raptures in the Bible?

Amir: Enoch and Elijah are known for the fact that they did not die but were taken up to heaven by God. Enoch is mentioned in the genealogy of Adam, in Genesis 5:24, which says, "Enoch walked with God, and he was not, for God took him." Hebrews 11:5 tells us that Enoch "had this testimony, that he pleased God," which is why he was taken.

We do not know how Enoch was taken—only why. In 2 Kings 2, however, we read that Elijah was also taken up by God, but this happened in front of an eyewitness, his understudy Elisha, who saw the chariot of God come for Elijah and take him to heaven in a whirlwind.

These two men were caught up to heaven in the same way the church is going to be caught up. We, too, are going to be taken for the same reason Enoch was—because we are "in Christ."

Barry: In a time when many people question the validity of the rapture of the church, it is good that we can look back to examples of other raptures to establish a precedent. It's not as though we believe in a phenomenon that has never happened before or is absent from the pages of Scripture. Outside of Enoch and Elijah, I believe we can find two other pictures of the rapture in the Old Testament, through what happened to Noah and Lot.

The apostle Peter tells us that Noah, a righteous man, and his family were lifted above God's wrath through the means of an ark. He then adds that Lot, a righteous man, was removed from the direct path of God's wrath before Sodom was destroyed (2 Peter 2:5-7). Some people will respond by saying, "But Noah and Lot never left the earth, so that means the church will go through the tribulation." But we need to remember that types or pictures are not exact matches with what will happen in the future, but rather, they are portrayals. Noah and Lot were both righteous men who had their physical location changed to remove them from the path of God's wrath.

As for Enoch and Elijah, though they were not removed from the direct path of God's wrath, they were taken to heaven because they were righteous. So again, the typologies of Noah, Lot, Enoch, and Elijah are like representative arrows that point to a future event even though they are not exactly the same.

Moses has been described as a type of Christ because he led God's people out of bondage. Joshua is seen as a type of Christ because he led God's people into the land of promise. Neither of these men were previous Christs—there is only one Lord Jesus Christ. But both men pointed to Christ, who is the fulfillment of all things. The two men combined paint a picture of what Jesus would do later. Similarly, Noah, Lot, Enoch, and Elijah paint a picture of the rapture of the church. None of them paint the perfect picture, but Noah and Lot tell us that God has, in the past, changed the location of His righteous ones to remove them from His wrath. And Enoch and Elijah inform us that God has, at times, bypassed death for those who please Him.

11. How can God rapture so many people all at once?

Barry: If God can speak all things into existence in six 24-hour night/day cycles, then taking two people or two billion people into heaven simultaneously is no harder for Him. The number of people who will be taken in the rapture is of no consequence in relation to God's ability to take them up. In fact, Jeremiah 32:17 tells us that as the maker of heaven and earth, nothing is too hard for God.

This brings up an important point: I am not one for Christian buzzwords or catchphrases, but there is one term that I have always thought to be appropriate for us to incorporate into our thinking, and that is the term *big God-er*. In other words, we should always be mindful of the greatness and majestic power of God. We can do this simply by remembering what the Bible tells us about Him—for example, He rides the clouds (Psalm 68:4), sits over the circle of the earth (Isaiah 40:22), names and numbers the stars (Psalm 147:4), sets the boundaries for the seas (Proverbs 8:29), raises up kings and sets them down (Daniel 2:21), there is none like Him (Jeremiah 10:6), He is the Lord of armies (Psalm 46:7 NASB), and He is the King of kings and the Lord of lords (1 Timothy 6:15). If we remember these truths, then the *how* questions will all find their place.

How can God rapture so many people at once? He is God.

Amir: We have so many examples of God's power being manifested in Scripture that this question should not even come into our minds. All we need to do is look at Jesus, and we will find the answer. He healed the sick, raised the dead, restored sight, made the lame walk, and twice He fed thousands of people with next to nothing.

Job 9:10 tells us that God does "great things past finding out" and "wonders without number." That means He can do more than our minds can imagine, and He does them without limitation. He can take Enoch and Elijah to heaven one at a time, or He can take an entire generation of living Christians and, at the same time, resurrect millions of the dead in Christ from throughout church history so they can meet Him in the air. So we do not need to wonder about how God is capable of rapturing so many people. We should see it as a wonder, yes, but we shouldn't concern ourselves over whether it is possible.

CHAPTER 4

THE TRIBULATION

THE TRIBULATION

At the conclusion of the church age will come the rapture, the removal of the bride of Christ from the earth. This will soon be followed by the tribulation—seven years of God's discipline against Israel and His wrath against the world.

Those of us who have given our lives to Jesus and received His forgiveness will not be part of the horrors of the tribulation. We are not destined for wrath. Jesus promised for those who "have kept My command to persevere, I also will keep you from the hour of trial which shall come upon the whole world, to test those who dwell on the earth" (Revelation 3:10). According to Jesus' words, for us to avoid the trial that will come upon the whole earth, we must no longer be among those who dwell on the earth. For that to happen, a supernatural act needs to take place. This can only happen by the hand of God:

The Lord Himself will descend from heaven with a shout, with the voice of an archangel, and with the trumpet of God. And the dead in Christ will rise first. Then we who are alive and remain shall be caught up together with them in the clouds to meet the Lord in the air. And thus we shall always be with the Lord. Therefore comfort one another with these words (1 Thessalonians 4:16-18).

That promise of being raptured before the tribulation is our comfort as we see those seven years approaching. Sadly, there are many people who will choose to endure the tribulation by rejecting Jesus' free offer of salvation through faith in Him. For those of us in the church, however, we will be in heaven—as stated in the passage above. We will be with our Savior. To be in His presence and see His face should be motivation enough for us to echo the words of the elderly apostle, writer, and friend of the Savior: "Even so, come, Lord Jesus!" (Revelation 22:20).[5]

1. Has the seven-year tribulation already begun?

Amir: I was in New York City when 9/11 took place. In fact, I was on top of the Twin Towers the night before. And during the days that followed, people were asking, "Was this God's judgment against America?"

When people asked me that, I said, "No, that was actually God's mercy, not God's judgment." Yes, many died, but many more could have died if all the attacks planned for that day had been carried out to their full extent. Besides, if you want to know what God's judgment looks like, then you need to think in terms of complete cities being wiped out, or fire coming down from heaven. If you want to see descriptions of God's judgment on a massive scale, read the book of Revelation.

The bad things taking place today do not compare to what will happen to this world during the tribulation. Judgment will be so severe that, as Jesus said in Matthew 24:22, "Unless those days were shortened, no flesh would be saved." This gives us some idea of just how terrible things will be.

COVID-19 had a devastating impact, but many people were still healthy, and to some extent, the world has recovered. While the virus was widespread, it still doesn't compare to the kind of devastation that will come from unprecedented earthquakes and brimstones falling from heaven. Nor have we seen anything like the sun scorching people with fire, as described in Revelation 16:8.

Right now, life on earth is a picnic compared to what will happen during the tribulation. You do *not* want to be here at that time. People will suffer so greatly that they want to die, but won't be able to. Can you imagine wanting to die and yet having death evade you? That's how bad life will get. Some people who reject Christ now say, "I'll take my chances. And if the tribulation really does happen, then I'll accept Jesus." But no one should think that way, for two reasons: We are told that many people will become so hardhearted that they still reject God, and we know that people will die in such large numbers that they might never have the opportunity to change their mind.

Barry: In John 16:33, Jesus said that in this life, we will have tribulation. Some people interpret this to mean that the church will go through the seven-year tribulation. The problem with this perspective is that the tribulation is a time of God's wrath, and 1 Thessalonians 5:9 says, "God did not appoint us to wrath, but to obtain salvation." Revelation 3:10 also offers a promise to those who persevere—that is, those who remain steadfast in the faith: They will be kept "from the hour of trial which shall come upon the whole world."

The biggest problem with thinking that the church will go through the tribulation is it denies the fact that Jesus bore the wrath of the Father when He died on the cross for our sins. This is why the church cannot go through the tribulation—Jesus has already taken onto Himself the wrath that was appointed to us. And the purposes of the tribulation are for God to pour out His wrath on an unbelieving world and to finish His discipline of Israel.

Simply put, the tribulation cannot have begun because the church is still here. Until Jesus comes for us, the tribulation we experience is the result of living in a fallen world and experiencing the wrath of people around us, not God's wrath. Jesus said we can respond to this kind of tribulation with good cheer because He has overcome the world (John 16:33). In contrast, there is nothing that the people who remain on earth during the tribulation can be cheery about.

2. Is there a connection between the white horse in Revelation 6 and the rise of the antichrist in Revelation 13?

Barry: Yes. Many people mistakenly think the rider on the white horse is Jesus because of the horse's color. In Revelation 19, we read that Jesus will return to earth on a white horse. However, there is no question that the rider in Revelation 6 is the same person as the beast in Revelation 13. One important clue is that the rider in Revelation 6 has a bow in his hand but no arrows, although some people say the arrows are implied. I do not agree with that for the simple reason that if you read the Greek translation of the Old Testament (the Septuagint), you will find the same Greek word used in Revelation 6 for "bow" is translated as "rainbow" in Genesis 9:13. There, the Lord set the rainbow in the clouds as a symbol of the covenant He made with all the earth not to flood the world again in judgment. That gives us an Old Testament precedence for a bow being symbolic of a covenant.

We know from Daniel 9:27 that the beast will make a seven-year covenant with Israel, and we know he will break that covenant in the middle of the seven years. This means the covenant has to be the "opening event" of the tribulation, and Revelation 6 describes the beginning of that seven-year period.

Another reason we know the rider in Revelation 6 is not Jesus but rather, the antichrist—who is also the first beast of Revelation 13—is because the second rider of the famed four horsemen of the apocalypse will take peace *away* from the earth. So the peace offered by the first rider will be short-lived. In contrast, when Jesus brings peace to the earth, it's going to last for 1,000 years.

Amir: We also must remember that there is no mention of the church in Revelation 6–19, and that Paul, in 2 Thessalonians 2:8, said that the lawless one—the rider on the white horse—cannot be revealed until the hindering work of the Holy Spirit is taken out of the way. Because Christians are the temple of the Holy Spirit, that means the church must be gone before the lawless one can ride onto the world scene and make his covenant with Israel.

Again, keep in mind that Revelation 6 presents the opening of the tribulation. And then Revelation 13 reveals details about the two men empowered by Satan who will deceive the world—that is, the antichrist and the false prophet. The book of Revelation is not entirely in chronological sequence, although the seal, trumpet, and bowl judgments do happen in the order that they are described. So the fact we see the antichrist mentioned in Revelation 13 doesn't mean that's the first time he appears in Revelation. We also see him in Revelation 6 on the white horse. That's when he first appears on the world scene with a covenant with Israel in hand.

3. Who are the 144,000 in Revelation 7?

Amir: Revelation 7 clearly states that the 144,000 are Jews from the 12 tribes of Israel. You may be aware that in the Old Testament, the lists of the 12 tribes appear multiple times, and the lists vary a bit. In Revelation 7, in the New Testament, we see that the tribe of Dan is not mentioned. But it does include Manasseh, who was Jacob's grandson.

Dan was probably omitted because the people abandoned their original allotted territory and moved to the northern end of the country. Also, the tribe of Dan was among the first to fall into idolatry. Even today, you'll find the ruins of a pagan altar at Tel Dan on Israel's northern border with Lebanon.

Though Manasseh is listed in place of Dan, we must remember that doesn't mean Dan has been cast off by God. He has not forsaken that tribe forever. In the book of Ezekiel, where we read about the territories that will be assigned to the tribes during the millennium, the tribe of Dan is listed first. This brings to mind what Paul wrote in Romans 11:1, where he said that God has "certainly not" cast away His people. This includes Dan.

Barry: Revelation 7 clearly states the identity of the 144,000, saying that it is comprised of 12,000 men from each of the 12 tribes of Israel. Revelation 14 adds that they have the name of the Father written on their foreheads (verse 1), they sing a song that only they know (verse 3), they are virgins who follow the Lamb wherever He goes (verse 4), and they are without fault before God (verse 5).

There is only one way to be without fault before God, and that is to be born again, even if you're a Jew. Revelation 14 also says that these virgins have not defiled themselves sexually with women, which tells us they are all males. Verse 4 affirms this fact again by saying they were "redeemed from among men." The reason they are all males is likely because they function in the role of priests or pastors during the tribulation, offices that are reserved exclusively for men. This may not be a popular point with many people today, but that doesn't make it untrue.

In summary, the 144,000 are sexually pure male Jews tasked with preaching the gospel, and they will be supernaturally protected as they carry out their commission.

4. When will the two witnesses of Revelation 11 appear?

Amir: The two witnesses will carry out their ministry during the first three-and-a-half years of the seven-year tribulation. They will be killed and taken to heaven at the halfway point, and then the ministry of the 144,000 will begin. They will proclaim the gospel around the world.

Because the church will be taken up to heaven before the tribulation, we will not see the two witnesses or the 144,000. God did not reveal the names of the two witnesses; if he wanted us to know who they will be, He would have done so. The two witnesses will definitely be active when the temple is standing on the Temple Mount. The Jewish people will believe that they are worshipping at the temple of God, and will not be aware that the one who signed a seven-year covenant with them will later turn on them, desecrate the temple, and declare himself to be God.

Many people have speculated about the identity of the two witnesses. I believe the best perspective to have is this: Where the Bible is silent, we should be silent.

Barry: It is interesting that the two witnesses will exercise gifts that are similar to those practiced by God's spokesmen in the Old Testament: shutting up the sky, calling down fire, and other activities we can expect to take place during the tribulation—the first half, to be specific. We should note that the technology necessary for the whole world to watch the two witnesses die, then rise to heaven, has only recently become available. We are now living in a day when it is possible for everyone all over the globe to simultaneously see what is happening at any given place.

I agree with Amir that when the Bible is silent about something, we ought to be silent as well. Yet I'll also say that there are many people who think Enoch and Elijah are likely to be the two witnesses because they never died. But those suggestions are basically invalidated by the fact that, at the rapture, there will be a whole generation of people who will have never tasted death and will be supernaturally translated into the presence of God. I believe we are that generation, so we need to be looking up as our redemption draws nigh. Who are the two witnesses? As Amir says, I believe it's best for us not to speculate.

5. Who is the primary audience of the two witnesses— Jews, Gentiles, or both?

Barry: Revelation 11 describes the ministry of the two witnesses, and in that chapter, we find imagery that is all specific to the Jewish people. The olive tree and lampstands from Zechariah 4, and the instruction in Revelation 11:2 not to measure the outer court because it has been given over to the Gentiles, seem to identify that the ministry of the two witnesses will be to the Jews. It is also very likely that they will be Jewish themselves—after all, their ministry will take place during the seventieth week of Daniel, and the 70 weeks are all part of God's dealings with Israel.

Amir: Yes, the two witnesses will minister to the Jewish people. Their actions are similar to those of the Hebrew prophets of old, and until their time is up, God will supernaturally protect them during their ministry—just as He will protect the Jews who will look on the One whom they pierced when Jesus returns at the second coming (Zechariah 12:10).

Revelation 11 makes it clear that the two witnesses' ministry will be known by the Gentiles. We are told in verse 9 that "those from the peoples, tribes, tongues, and nations will see their dead bodies three-and-a-half days" (verse 9), and they will rejoice over their deaths. The whole world will know about them, and their ministry will have an impact on some who will come to believe among the Gentiles. But the primary focus of their ministry will be the Jews,

6. **According to Daniel 12:1, the tribulation will be a time of distress like the world has never seen. Does this refer to all seven years of the tribulation, or just the second half?**

Amir: The entire tribulation is a time of God's wrath. Daniel himself talks about "the latter time of the indignation" (Daniel 8:19) when he speaks of the latter part of the wrath. But the entire seven years is a time of God's wrath. During the first three-and-a-half years, the Jews will be blinded. This will be a time of testing, and they will agree to a seven-year covenant with the one who will allow them to build their temple. However, the moment he declares himself to be God, there will be some Jews who say, "No, you're not!" That's when the antichrist will start persecuting them, and, of course, these Jews will flee to the desert, where they will be protected for 1,260 days, according to Revelation 12:6.

Some people suggest that "the time of trouble" refers only to the antichrist's persecution of Israel, and not the whole world. Yes, Israel will have a hard time from day one of the tribulation, which we can see just by reading about the judgments sent by the two witnesses. But the whole world will experience the horrors of the four horsemen of the apocalypse, not just the Jews. These horsemen will be released right at the start of the tribulation (Revelation 6:1-9).

But the minute the Jewish people see that this man who made a covenant with them is calling himself God, they will reject him—at least those who desire to stay faithful to God. And they will flee to the desert to escape his persecution.

Barry: There is, without question, a transition at the midpoint of the tribulation, but it is not a transition from pseudo peace to wrath. There are those who say that the four horsemen of the apocalypse in Revelation 6 won't appear until the second half of the tribulation. The main difficulty with that interpretation is that there is nothing in Revelation 6 to indicate that.

The first rider, on the white horse, will emerge onto the world scene with a covenant in hand and conquer the world. The second rider will then take the false peace from the earth and people will begin to butcher each other. The third rider will introduce global famine, and the fourth rider will kill a quarter of the world's population by sword, hunger, death, and the beasts of the earth.

Remember that there is no mention of the church from Revelation chapter 6 to chapter 19. We know that the church will be absent from the earth during this time. However, there will be saints on the earth from every tribe, tongue, nation, and people, and they are introduced to us as martyrs at the opening of the fifth seal in Revelation 6:9-11.

This, as well as other events, will happen during the initial phase of the tribulation, or the first 1,260 days. The first five seals unveil what I call the consequential wrath of God. The deceitful and evil hearts of humanity will be manifest in the brutality and greed expressed by everyone when the four horsemen are released. The cataclysmic wrath of God begins at the opening of the sixth seal, when an earthquake strikes and the sun and moon are darkened. The people of the earth will then hide in the rocks and caves and cry out, "Fall on us and hide us from the face of Him who sits on the throne and from the wrath of the Lamb! For the great day of His wrath has come, and who is able to stand?" (verses 16-17).

The entire seven years is a time of God's wrath. It will begin when God no longer restrains the antichrist's rise to power. That, too, will be an act of God's wrath.

7. When the Holy Spirit is removed, which will allow the antichrist to rise to power, how will people become saved?

Barry: There are two key truths to remember about the tribulation: First, Revelation 7:9 speaks of a multitude from "all nations, tribes, peoples, and tongues, standing before the throne and before the Lamb, clothed with white robes." These will be the tribulation martyrs—those who are slain for their faith during the tribulation. Second, Jesus said in John 6:44, "No one can come to Me unless the Father who sent Me draws him." In these ways, we can know that people will definitely come to salvation during the tribulation. Getting saved during that time will happen the same way it does now—through the blood of Jesus washing away our sin and making us clean.

Also, the tribulation is the seventieth week of Daniel. During that time, the focus will be on Daniel's people and the holy city, meaning the Jews and Jerusalem (Daniel 9:24). The church will be gone, which means all the people who were privileged to be temples of the Holy Spirit will have been removed from earth. God will then work as He did during Old Testament times—He will draw people to Himself, and the Holy Spirit will come "upon" people as He did in Old Testament days. He will be present and active on the earth as He was during the first 69 weeks, before the church age.

During the tribulation, people will still become saved by the conviction of the Holy Spirit. The Father will draw people to Jesus, whose blood will cleanse them of their sin. It is wrong to assume the Holy Spirit's work on earth is "deactivated" during the tribulation. He will still do His work, but in the same way He did in Old Testament times rather than during the church age.

Amir: The Holy Spirit is God, equal to the Father and the Son. That means He is omnipresent—He is everywhere all the time. This means it is not possible for His presence to be absent from the earth during the tribulation.

When Paul talked about the restrainer being taken out of the way in 2 Thessalonians 2:7, he was making two points: He was saying that the purifying and preserving influence of the church that has been holding back utter lawlessness on the earth will be removed, and the hindering force of the Holy Spirit—which has kept the antichrist from rising to power—will be taken out of the way. Even though the church will have been removed through the rapture, the Spirit of God will still be present and active because He is God, and He is omnipresent.

8. After the rapture, how will world leaders address the fact that millions of people are missing?

Amir: I don't know, but what I do know is that the most important priority a person can have right now is to make sure he or she doesn't miss the rapture. I am sure there will be plenty of explanations offered as to why so many people are missing, but Scripture doesn't reveal that information. Jesus said to be ready, for He is coming at a time when people don't expect (Matthew 24:44). If He said to be ready, then we need to be ready.

Paul also told us in 1 Corinthians 15:52 that the rapture will happen in a twinkling of an eye. In 1 Thessalonians 4:16, he said the dead in Christ will rise first, then the believers who are alive will meet them in the air. This means world leaders will have to come up with an explanation not only for why so many people are missing, but also why there are millions of empty graves.

I am sure that whatever leaders say, the people of the world will believe them. There are already many people who view Christians in a negative light. So we shouldn't be surprised if, after the rapture, leaders say that the world will be a better place because all the Christians are gone.

Barry: The Bible does not reveal the explanations that will be given after the rapture, but we can make some calculated guesses based on some facts we do know. One key point is that some will realize that everyone who disappeared shared a common trait: They were born-again Christians. From what we can tell, those who are left will not all suddenly decide to repent and believe on the Lord Jesus Christ. That may mean the people who are left will already have been pre-conditioned to believe lies.

That's important because all the explanations that world leaders give will have to be lies. They won't want to admit Christians were right, and more importantly, during the tribulation, the father of lies (John 8:44) will be in control of the world like never before. The beast and the false prophet of Revelation 13 will both be purveyors of the lies that will be offered as explanations for why so many people disappeared all at once. The last thing they will want to admit is the truth.

It is also noteworthy that people around the world have been introduced to the concept of a "cosmic cleansing" or "internal cleansing" through Taoism, Hinduism, and the New Age movement. This concept teaches that because we are one with the universe, we can experience an internal cleansing through meditation and other practices. On a grander scale, there is the idea that a self-creating universe can also cleanse itself of undesirables.

Astronomers have long reported that the universe is self-cleansing of certain energy fields and sources. It is possible that some will take this idea and say that because we, as humans, are one with the universe, the universe has cleansed itself of undesirable humans.

Whatever the explanation offered, the lie will be viewed by much of the world as a positive step forward. And that, in turn, will make it all the easier for people everywhere to go along with the execution of all the undesirables who refuse the mark of the beast.

The Bible doesn't say how people will explain away the rapture, but we do know the world will succumb to deception and lies like never before.

9. Do we know the nationality of the antichrist?

Barry: Scripture reveals to us a general geographic region—we know that he will rise from some form of revived Roman Empire. Some have made a case that because Antiochus Epiphanes, who is a type of the antichrist, was Greek, that the antichrist could be Greek. Others believe that because Micah 5:5 mentions an Assyrian coming "into their land," this implies he will be a Muslim. This is beyond unlikely, for the Jews will make a covenant with the antichrist and follow him for a while, and they would never follow a Muslim, and the Muslims would never agree to let the Jews rebuild the temple.

I don't believe we can say definitively what nationality the antichrist will be. All we know is the geographic region he will rise up from. According to Revelation 17, he will bring together a coalition of leaders around him. They're going to seek to dominate the world during the tribulation period. The statue in Daniel chapter 2 has legs of iron, which we know to be the ancient Roman Empire, which was split into two. Then the feet and ten toes are made partly of iron, which represents the territories of the Roman Empire, and partly of clay, which speaks of other nations forming a weak and fragile coalition. These are the clues we have that indicate the antichrist will rise from somewhere in the revived Roman Empire.

Amir: When Daniel talks about the antichrist, it is in the same breath that he talks about the empire that will destroy the temple in AD 70—the Romans. We know that the visions that Daniel had are consistent with the visions that John described in Revelation with regard to the region of the world the antichrist will come from. I have no doubt he's going to come from Western Europe. In fact, I've taught two messages on this. One is "Europe Ready for the Antichrist" and the other is "Europe Closer to the Antichrist." I believe he's going to come from that region.

Now, some people point to current world leaders and wonder if they might be the antichrist, but as we already know, the antichrist will not be revealed until after the restrainer, or Holy Spirit, has been taken away. So the antichrist won't be known until after the rapture, and when the tribulation begins. For this reason, there is no sense in trying to identify a current world leader as being the antichrist.

We should not speculate, and we know the church will not be on earth when the antichrist rises to power. What we do know is that he will rise up from where the Roman Empire used to be 2,000 years ago.

10. What is the abomination of desolation, and when will it take place?

Barry: We mentioned Antiochus Epiphanes as being a type of the antichrist. This man, who has many parallels to the man of sin in the tribulation, violated the most holy place in the Jewish temple. One way he was a type of the coming antichrist is that he minted coins with his image and the inscription "King Antiochus, God Manifest." The antichrist will claim to be God as well. Antiochus erected a statue of Zeus and sacrificed a pig on the altar in the Holy of Holies, and the antichrist will have an image of himself erected in the temple and demand that he be worshipped.

In the Olivet Discourse, Jesus said that the abomination of

desolation will occur when the antichrist stands in the holy place (Matthew 24:15), where he shouldn't be. The statute of Zeus also was put in a place where it shouldn't be. Second Thessalonians 2:4 says the antichrist will sit in the temple and declare himself to be God. All of this tells us that there will be a third temple (which is implied in Scripture, and not directly stated), and that the antichrist will use the temple to glorify himself as God.

So we can conclude that the temple will be built during the tribulation and not before, for the only way the antichrist could have access to the most holy place is for him to be in control of the structure. And the covenant the antichrist makes with Israel will most likely make it possible for the temple to be rebuilt.

Amir: The third temple is not for the Messiah, it is for the antichrist. That means the temple we read about in Ezekiel 40 and beyond, in the millennium, will be the fourth temple. The third temple, in which the abomination of desolation will take place, is part of the covenantal agreement the antichrist makes with Israel. Daniel 9:27 says that at the midpoint of the seven-year covenant, the antichrist will bring an end to the sacrifices and offerings of Israel and commit the abomination of desolation.

In Matthew 24:15, Jesus said that when the Jews see the antichrist desecrate the temple, they are to flee to the mountains and not go back to take anything from their houses. The Bible tells us repeatedly that the tribulation will last for two periods of 42 months, or 1,260 days each. The abomination of desolation, when the antichrist declares himself to be God, will occur at the midpoint of the tribulation. Revelation does not report the actual event, but it seems that chapter 13, where we read specifics about the beast and the false prophet, is followed by the bowl judgments, which include the undiluted wrath of God on the antichrist's kingdom. Revelation 15:1

says that in the bowl judgments, "the wrath of God is complete." This is the most likely time when the abomination of desolation will occur in the chronological sequence of Revelation.

11. How is it that the Jews will know where to flee at the midpoint of the tribulation?

Amir: There won't be many options available. In fact, there will be only one place, and Revelation 12:6 tells us it will be "prepared by God." God has already determined this location and will have made it ready long before it is needed. It's very possible that those who want to flee will somehow hear about this place. For example, the two witnesses might say, "If you refuse to bow down to the antichrist, there is a place that God has prepared for you."

We don't know how the message will get out about this place. But we do know God has prepared it, and that those who flee will run to it. So somehow, the information will be communicated to them.

One of the elders at my church said that during the 1960s, there was a group of believers who came to Jerusalem on an unusual mission. At that time, the eastern part of Jerusalem was still in the hands of Jordan. These believers crossed into the Jordanian side of Jerusalem and took a bus to Petra, a place with cliffs that have many caves. Apparently, they hid hundreds of Hebrew-language Bibles in the caves. They hoped that when the Jewish people flee to Petra during the tribulation, they will then read about the Messiah whom they have rejected so far. This will enable them to know exactly who the Messiah is when He comes.

How will the Jewish people know where to go when the

abomination of desolation occurs? We're not told, but we can assume that at the time they need to know, the details will be given to them.

Barry: The 70-weeks prophecy in Daniel has to do with the Jewish people, which includes the final week, or seventieth week, also known as the tribulation. So this is a time during which God will deal with Israel again, as He has done in times past. You'll remember that when the people of Israel were wandering in the wilderness, God directed them by a pillar of fire by night and a pillar of cloud by day. It is possible that when the Jewish people need to flee the abomination of desolation, God will use some supernatural means to direct them to their destination.

When we think about the tribulation, our minds are quick to go to all the cataclysmic events described in the book of Revelation. But we need to remember that it will also be a time of incredible supernatural activity as well. For example, there will be 144,000 specially protected Jews preaching the gospel, two Old Testament prophet-like witnesses with miraculous powers, and an angel flying in the air proclaiming the everlasting gospel. There will be an abundance of supernatural activity and direction during this time.

Amir mentioned those Hebrew-language Bibles that were hidden in the caves in Petra. The Jews who flee may very well read the Bible in a new way as a result of what they witness happening around them. God will use whatever means He needs to use to reach the Jewish people with the gospel.

With all the supernatural activity that is described in the book of Revelation, I would imagine that God will devise a way to let the fleeing Jews know where to go for protection. God has guided His people in the past, and He will do so again in the future.

12. When does the revived Roman Empire come about—before the tribulation, or after the tribulation begins?

Amir: Definitely after. As 2 Thessalonians 2 says, the Holy Spirit acts as a hindering force that prevents the lawless one's rise to power. The Spirit must first be taken out of the way. This will happen at the rapture, when all the people who comprise the church are taken away, along with the indwelling Spirit. It's not until the church is taken out of the way that the antichrist will establish his seven-year covenant with Israel. And if the antichrist can't rise to power until after the rapture, then he cannot establish the ten-nation coalition described in Daniel 2 and Revelation 17 before the rapture.

That doesn't mean that we are not moving in the direction of the creation of the revived Roman Empire. In the same way that we are seeing the preparations for the Ezekiel 38 war come about, we are seeing developments that will lead to the revived Roman Empire. The European Union is certainly a step in that direction, as well as the globalist agenda of the progressive left. The fact the revived Roman Empire won't be fully formed until after the rapture does not mean nothing will happen before the rapture. Developments are taking place now that are leading us in that direction.

In some ways, the recent pandemic has brought about a unity that the world has never seen. There is a single source or voice that is dictating world policies, and that is the World Health Organization, in cooperation with the CDC (Centers for Disease Control and Prevention) and the National Institutes of Health. Nations are still acting independently, but leaders have been working together to figure out how to respond to the pandemic. This has normalized the concept of having a few powerful people govern over what is done in many countries. Everything is moving in a direction that will make it easier for the antichrist to rise to power after the church is gone.

Barry: Revelation 17:12 says that the ten heads who rule with the antichrist will do so "for one hour," meaning a short time. The same verse also tells us these leaders "have received no kingdom as yet." That informs us that the geopolitical landscape of the world is going to change after the rapture. That which the world is being primed for in the future, the world will be ready and even hungry for after the rapture.

The fact that Revelation 17:12 tells us that the ten kings— or political powers or heads of state—have not received a kingdom as of yet tells us it is possible that the current world leaders will not be included in the antichrist's global regime, so speculation about who these leaders are is pointless.

Revelation 17:13 goes on to say these leaders are of one mind with the beast, "and they will give their power and authority to the beast. These will make war with the Lamb, and the Lamb will overcome them, for He is the Lord of lords and King of kings"—that is, Jesus.

We don't know who the antichrist is, and we don't know the identities of the ten kings who will rule with him for the short time of his reign. But we do know who will defeat all of them: the King of kings and Lord of lords. Revelation 19:11-16 is one of my favorite Bible passages. This passage reminds us that Jesus is no longer a helpless child in a manger, and He is no longer a bloodied and innocent Passover lamb. He will return to fight against His enemies as the Lion of Judah, the faithful and true One who judges and makes war.

Neither ten kings nor 10,000 kings can defeat Him, for He is the King above all kings and Lord above all lords. Someday, every knee will bow and every tongue will confess that He is Lord (Philippians 2:10-11), including those who joined the antichrist's armies to fight against Christ when He returned.

13. What does it mean in Revelation 12:9 that Satan was "cast to the earth" and that he knows "he has a short time"?

Barry: This is an interesting question that has led people to come up with different answers. The word "cast" means "to be thrown down," which implies an act of force, but it can also mean "to be put in a lower place." I think we can arrive at a solid understanding of this passage by using the latter meaning to establish our interpretation. Does this mean Satan was thrown out of heaven and sent to the earth? The text actually says Satan *came* down, not that he was *thrown* down to the earth.

We know from the book of Job that Satan has access to the presence of God, even after he fell initially, as Jesus stated in Luke 10:18. The word "fall" in Luke means "to fall under judgment." This is when iniquity was found in Satan and he fell out of favor with God. This is separate from what Revelation 12 describes, and I believe that the most sensible interpretation of Revelation 12:9 is that Satan was cut off from the presence of God and was put in a lower place. His reaction was to come down to the earth, which again indicates he still had access to heaven (as recorded in Job), and he did this knowing that he had little time left to carry out his agenda against the Jews and God-fearing Gentiles.

Amir: I believe that even in heaven there are realms, much like there are high mountains and lower mountains here on earth. And

I don't believe Satan was thrown down to earth per se, but that his fall, whenever it was, was like lightning (Luke 10:18). But in Revelation, we see something different. At this time the church is in heaven, and the antichrist has risen to power on earth. At the midpoint of the tribulation, when the antichrist sits in the most holy place and declares himself to be God, the true and living God will say, "That's it!" And Satan will be thrown down to a lower place, no longer having access to the throne room of God.

I call this the great exchange—the church will go up and Satan will come down. I find this amazing, for the reason we will be raptured is so that Jesus can keep us away from the literal rule of Satan on earth. For now, Satan is just the prince of the power of the air (Ephesians 2:2), and he is the father of all lies (John 8:44). Someday, he will go from ruling in the spiritual realm to ruling physically on earth. The antichrist will receive his seat, his power, and his authority from the dragon, along with all the false signs and wonders that the dragon will empower him to do, which he will use to deceive the whole world. All of this will create a truly horrific situation on earth.

Can you imagine becoming a believer during the time when Satan's presence on earth is so overwhelming and he knows he has only a short amount of time left? Thankfully, we are not destined to face the wrath of God. We won't be here. The church must first be removed for the antichrist to be revealed.

14. Does Armageddon happen before the tribulation?

Amir: Before I answer that, I want to say there is no place in the Bible that specifically says "the battle of Armageddon." If you find it, I'll pay for your trip to Israel. What we do read is that Revelation 16:16 says, "They gathered them [their forces] together to the place called in Hebrew, Armageddon," or *Har Megiddo*, which means "the gathering place." This area is real; I see it every day that I am at home. It is right outside my door. But the war that the "Armageddon gathering" is all about will take place in Jerusalem.

Zechariah chapters 12, 13, and 14 are about that war, which will end with the return of Jesus to the earth. He will come back—and we will be with Him—to judge the nations, divide the sheep from the goats, and establish His millennial kingdom.

As we consider the tribulation, we need to remember that the first 1,260 days (42 months) are for the two witnesses—that's the first three-and-a-half years. During the last 42 months, or the last three-and-a-half years, the nations will tread the holy city underfoot (Revelation 11:2) because the Jews are gone. They will have fled to the desert, as Revelation 12 tells us.

So yes, Armageddon is the gathering place. It will take place at the end of the tribulation, and it will kick off the war that will eventually end at Jerusalem. The Jews will come back, and Jesus will have set His feet on the Mount of Olives. We will be with Him, and He will fight against Israel's enemies, and of course He will win.

Barry: I am not sure why there is so much confusion surrounding the war in Ezekiel 38–39 and the final battle described in Zechariah 12 and Revelation 19. These two events feature different combatants and different battle theaters, and there is no mention of burying the dead or burning weapons in the final battle, so the two must be distinct from one another.

The conflict that many people commonly refer to as the battle of Armageddon is the one in which, as Zechariah 14:3 says, "the LORD will go forth and fight against those nations, as He fights in the day of battle." This clearly parallels Revelation 19:11-16, where the Lord comes to make war and wears a robe dipped in blood, and His name is called "the Word of God" (verse 13). Verse 16 says He has His name written on His robe and on His thigh, which is where ancient cavalrymen would wear the crest of the kingdom they were fighting for so they could be distinguished in the heat of battle.

Jesus' name being written in those places tells us He will come to fight in and for His own name and kingdom. While it is true that the Lord is the one who will bring the Ezekiel war to an end, the means by which "the battle of the great day of God Almighty" (which is how Revelation 16:14 refers to the campaign that begins at Armageddon) will end is completely different. In Ezekiel, the dead will lay on the mountains of Israel. In contrast, Zechariah 14:12 tells us that in the last battle, all those who fight against the Lord and Jerusalem will have their skin dissolve while they stand, their eyes dissolve in their sockets, and their tongues dissolve in their mouths. Zechariah 14 then goes on to talk about how the Feast of Tabernacles will be observed during the millennium (verse 16), which clearly indicates that the preceding battle scene has to do with the armies who gather at Armageddon and not the Ezekiel war.

15. What will happen to teenagers or children who are left behind when their believing parents are raptured—that is, those who have reached the age of accountability?

Barry: In our attempt to answer this question, we have to look to the clear teachings of Scripture to help interpret that which is unclear. What is the age of accountability? Does the Bible give us a specific answer?

Some say that because Paul says in 1 Corinthians 7:14 that

children are holy because of a believing parent in the home, young children of believers will be taken up in the rapture, while the children of nonbelievers will not. This conclusion falls outside of the context of what Paul talks about in the chapter and ignores the fact Paul was dealing with a specific issue in the city of Corinth: Married Christians were divorcing their unbelieving mates because they feared that marriage to an unbeliever defiled their home. But Paul said no—in actuality, the unbelieving spouse is sanctified because of the presence of the believing mate. When a believer dwells in the home, that home is sanctified, or set apart, because of the believer's presence.

This is what Paul meant when he said the children in such a home are holy. They are under the divine protection and blessings within the home because of the believing parent, even if the other parent is an unbeliever.

What we can know from a plain understanding of Scripture—an understanding that does not require any interpretive gymnastics—is that when the son born to David and Bathsheba died, David said he could not bring him back: "I shall go to him, but he shall not return to me" (2 Samuel 12:23). David understood that young children go to be with the Lord when they die.

When we ask about what will happen to children and teenagers at the rapture, we must consider the heart, nature, and character of God. The idea that God would leave children behind without parents during the tribulation—children who are too young to understand the gospel message or to care for themselves—goes against everything we know about God. In the times when we're trying to answer a tough question that isn't specifically addressed in Scripture, we have to fall back on what Abraham said when he negotiated with God over Sodom in Genesis 18: "Shall not the Judge of all the earth do right?" (verse 25).

What's sad is when young people are old enough to understand the simple message of the gospel yet don't respond to it. It would be just as wrong for God to rapture those who understand yet reject the gospel as it would be for Him to leave behind those who don't yet understand.

Amir: Yes, the heart of God is the right place to find an answer to this question—especially as we consider what we know about the Lord's love for children. In Matthew 19:14, Jesus said, "Let the little children come to Me, and do not forbid them; for of such is the kingdom of heaven." When He said that, He did not specify that they had to come from a Bible-believing home, and that if they don't, stay away from them and don't talk to them. He said this about all children.

I believe that, in general, God will be merciful to helpless children who are not yet mature enough to make decisions about life, and make sure that they are gathered to Him when He comes for His church. In Matthew 18:3, Jesus said that "unless you…become as little children, you will by no means enter the kingdom of heaven." If Jesus is using children as an example in this way, then we can safely assume that children who are under the age of understanding will be taken in the rapture.

Whatever the case may be, we know with certainty that God is fair, and He will do what is right.

16. Is the temple described in Ezekiel 40–48 the temple of the tribulation or the millennium?

Amir: It is absolutely the fourth temple, from which Jesus will rule during His 1,000-year reign on earth. Ezekiel 40–48 gives many details about the measurements, occupants, and offerings and sacrifices of this temple. In Ezekiel 47, we read about one specific detail that makes it clear this is the temple of the millennium and not that of the tribulation: healing waters will flow from the temple, and will be deep enough that one will need to swim in it to cross through (verse 5).

This matches what we read in Zechariah 14, which tells us about what will happen when Jesus returns to the earth. His feet will touch down on the Mount of Olives, and "living waters shall flow from Jerusalem" (verse 8).

Additional confirmation is found in Zechariah 14:9, which says this water will flow at a time when the Lord is King over all the earth. That is clearly a reference to the millennium and not the tribulation.

Going back to Ezekiel 47, we read about the dividing of the land as an inheritance to the 12 tribes of Israel (verses 13-23). Again, this tells us the context is the millennium. During the tribulation, the Jews will be fleeing for their lives because their temple has been desecrated, and there will be no healing waters. Instead, the world will experience the severest period of catastrophes and deaths ever.

For these reasons, we know that the temple in Ezekiel 40–48 is absolutely the millennial temple, and not the tribulation temple.

Barry: There is an interesting fact about the third temple that we cannot overlook: It is never actually described or even identified as such in Scripture. Rather, it is only implied. For the abomination of desolation to happen in the most holy place, we know there has to be a third temple. That's where the antichrist will declare himself to be God (2 Thessalonians 2:4). In Daniel 11:31, we read that during the antichrist's reign of terror, he will "take away the daily sacrifices, and place there the abomination of desolation." This is yet another clue that implies the future existence of the third temple without actually mentioning it.

A key distinction about the third temple is that it will not be God's temple, but the antichrist's. It will be a temple built by man for a man—one who deceives Israel and the world into thinking he is some kind of messianic figure who has the answer to the world's problems, including the ongoing Middle East crisis. He will allow the Jews to rebuild their temple, and then he will desecrate it. This will open some people's eyes to his false claims and true intentions.

Jesus said in Matthew 24:15-17 that when the beast commits the abomination of desolation, the Jews are to run for their lives and not even go back into the houses to grab their clothes because the antichrist's act will signal the onset of the worst time of tribulation the world has ever seen. This is exactly the opposite of what Ezekiel says about the fourth temple, which will be a place of true worship, healing, and peace—not war, terror, and tribulation.

17. Is the antichrist alive now?

Barry: I believe it is reasonable to assume that he is, but that's just an assumption. The way the world is being prepared for him to assume his role seems to be in process now. People are becoming conditioned to accept government mandates over their lives (including who can buy and sell), lawlessness is abounding, the love of many has grown cold, most of the church will not endure sound doctrine, and perilous times have come. The tribulation will last only seven years, and because the antichrist is called "the man of sin" (2 Thessalonians 2:3), and because wickedness is very much on the increase, it seems as though the world is becoming more prepared than ever for his arrival. So it's possible he is alive now.

In Daniel 11:21-23, we read about a type of the antichrist, a man named Antiochus Epiphanies. It is said that he rose from obscurity, without "the honor of royalty," and he came to power without warning and subdued the kingdom "by intrigue" (a phrase also associated with the antichrist). This tells us that the man of sin, the son of perdition, the first beast of Revelation 13 will rise to power in the same way. We do not, nor does anyone else, know who he is. He will rise out of nowhere and, with flattering speech, deceive the world into following him. The world is ready and primed for such a man, which is why I believe that it is probable he is alive today.

Amir: I agree it is likely that the antichrist is alive today and the world is being readied for him to take over. Two key pieces of the puzzle fell into place recently when the world's longest-running modern-day superpower, the United States, and the Middle East's only democracy, Israel, both opted for governments of change where lawlessness, under the banner of cultural sensitivities, replaced governments that sought to protect and defend the nation's identity and prosperity.

We live in a day in which many people believe a socialistic or communist form of government offers solutions to the world's problems—that is, a system in which the government assumes the role of God and is the provider of people's needs. This is what the antichrist will advocate, and if this is what everyone wants, and if governments are moving toward having one man lead the world, then he must be alive so that when the time comes, he will be ready to take his place of power.

We don't know who he is, but we do know he will arise from a revived form of the Roman Empire, according to Daniel 2 and

8. With the formation of the EU as a unified voice for the geographic region that made up the ancient Roman Empire, we have yet another indicator that it's likely the antichrist is alive now.

18. What will the church be doing in heaven while the tribulation is happening on earth?

Amir: There are three future judgments mentioned in the Bible: the judgment (or *bema*) seat of Christ, the judgment of the sheep and the goats, and the Great White Throne judgment. The *bema* seat is not a seat of judgment in the sense of determining one's eternal destiny, like the sheep and goats judgment, nor is it a final judgment, where people will be sent to hell, like the Great White Throne judgment. No one who stands at the *bema* seat of Christ will end up in hell.

The judgment seat of Christ, which Paul said all believers will stand before in 2 Corinthians 5:10, will take place in heaven while people on earth are experiencing God's wrath during the tribulation. We will not be judged with regard to our belief, but rather, for our works. In 1 Corinthians 3:12-13, Paul said our works will be tested by fire to see of what sort they are. And not only will we stand before the Lord and have our works recounted before Him, but our motives for those works will be judged as well. If the works in our lives were for self-promotion or personal gain, they will be burned up, yet we will remain saved. And if we build on the foundation of Christ with gold, silver, or precious stones, which are symbolic of pure motives, and our works survive the refining fire of Christ's judgment, we will receive a reward.

There are too many teachers today who downplay the importance of works in the life of a Christian. They view works as an infringement upon being saved by grace through faith. However, we're not saying that works are the *cause* of salvation, but rather, the *result* of it. Those who downplay the believer's works stop too soon in their reading of Ephesians 2: Yes, we are saved by grace through faith (verses 8-9), but the grace that saves us will move us to do good works (verse 10). It is sad that some Christians will stand before the Lord someday having done nothing to expand His kingdom. Ephesians 2:10 says "God prepared beforehand" for us to do "good works," and "we should walk in them." These works will be judged by the Lord Himself at the *bema* seat before we return with Him to earth at the second coming.

Barry: This is a matter of some debate, as some people see the stages of the Jewish wedding—the betrothal, the ceremony, and the sup-per—as a model for the progression of the church's place as the bride of Christ. We are in the betrothal stage right now, legally married to the groom, awaiting the Father's instruction to His Son to bring His bride to the Father's house for the wedding ceremony. The wedding supper, because of its mention directly before the second coming, is seen by some as taking place on earth. This seems unlikely, how-ever, in that what happens after the mention of the wedding supper of the Lamb and the blessings upon those who are called to it (the bride of Christ) is indeed a supper, but not for a wedding.

This feast is for the flesh-eating birds of the earth after the Son of Man returns in righteousness and judges His enemies (Revelation 19:11-16). This is *not* the celebratory scene of a wedding sup-per. So I agree with Amir—the wedding ceremony and supper will take place in heaven.

What we do know for sure is that while hell is breaking loose on earth, believers will be standing before the judgment seat of Christ in heaven (2 Corinthians 5:10). With that in mind, we should remember that Jesus taught two parables about rewards: the parable of the talents in Matthew 25, and the parable of the minas in Luke 19. A talent and a mina are both measures of weight. In the parables, these measures are obviously representative of the responsibility that has been entrusted to us for the work of expanding the Lord's kingdom. Those who do much with what their master gave them will receive much, and those who did nothing with what they were given will have it taken away and given to another.

There are a multitude of lessons in these parables, but in relation to the question above, it seems legitimate to say that when we stand before the Lord, we will be rewarded for what we did with what He entrusted to us. This reward will be reflected in the level of responsibilities we are given to handle during the millennium. In the parable of the minas, the rewards to the faithful were the privilege of ruling over a number of cities (Luke 19:17-18).

It is possible, then, that at the judgment seat of Christ, we will receive our assignments for reigning with Him during the millennium. Our works done on earth will be tested by fire. Works of wood, hay, and stubble—that is, those that are worthless or done for self-promotion—will be burned up. Works of gold, silver, and precious stones represent things done for God's glory and will be rewarded. The knowledge we will appear before the judgment seat of Christ should stir us to do works that bring glory to God.

19. Does the Old Testament mention the second coming of Jesus, or only His first coming?

Barry: This question underscores the importance of studying the whole Bible and not just the New Testament. If we attempt to cite Old Testament chapters and verses that say the Messiah is coming twice, we will not find any. What we *will* find is the necessity of His two comings, which is implied by what is written about the Messiah's activities here on earth.

The well-known Christmas prophecy of Isaiah 9:6-7 is a perfect example. It tells of a Child born and Son given, and it also speaks of the government being on His shoulder. That means that the Child born and Son given is someday going to rule the world, which He has yet to do—and thus the second coming is implied. Daniel 7:13-14 speaks of the Son of Man having dominion over all the earth. This, too, can only be fulfilled through the second coming of Christ, for the purpose of His first advent was to die for the sins of the world.

The necessity of a second coming was also revealed when the disciples, after Jesus' resurrection, asked Him if He was, at this time, going to restore the kingdom to Israel (Acts 1:6). The fact that there was no New Testament when they posed this question means they clearly understood that the Messiah would have dominion over the earth and that Israel would be restored to its former glory.

Yes, the Old Testament clearly teaches the second coming without using the phrase, much like the New Testament teaches the rapture without using the word. Christ's return is clearly implied.

Amir: Zechariah chapters 12–14 make it clear that Jesus is coming back to the earth a second time. In Zechariah 12:10, we see the inhabitants of Jerusalem look upon the one whom they pierced and respond by mourning. In Zechariah 14:4, we read that the Messiah's feet will touch down on the Mount of Olives, and later in verse 16, we're told all the nations of the earth will come up to Jerusalem to worship the King. Jesus has to come back in order for these events to occur.

In the Old Testament, we find prophecies about Jesus' first

coming, ministry, death, resurrection, ascension, taking up of the church, return with the church, rule with the saints, and conquest over Satan at the end of the millennium. The Passover pointed to Jesus' death, the Feast of Unleavened Bread pointed to Jesus' sinless life, the Feast of Firstfruits signified His resurrection from the dead, the Feast of Weeks or Pentecost pointed to the new covenant (which would yield a harvest of souls among Jews and Gentiles), the Feast of Trumpets points to Jesus' second coming, the Day of Atonement points to when Jesus divides the sheep from the goats, and the Feast of Tabernacles prefigures the millennial reign of Jesus on earth.

Does the Old Testament mention the second coming of Jesus? Yes! Jesus is mentioned all through the Old Testament because both testaments are about Him!

THE MILLENNIUM

THE MILLENNIUM

The millennium will be a literal kingdom in which Christ reigns for 1,000 years from a physical throne in Jerusalem. There will literally be actual changes in the physical realm, the spiritual realm, and the natural realm. I use the word *literally* on purpose because the changes are spelled out to us in the Word of God—spoken of by the prophets and witnessed by the apostle John.

Touch your arm. Do you feel the physicality of your body? Tap your foot on the ground. Do you sense the solid mass of the floor below you? Step outside. Do you feel the breeze that may be wisping across your face and gently flowing through your hair? Do you see the genuine nature of the landscape around you? That is because you are a real person living in a real world.

That is the same reality you will experience during the millennium. It's possible that our skin will feel a little different in our incorruptible bodies. It's likely the landscape will have changed some as a result of the devastation that took place during the tribulation. However, when those 1,000 years begin, you and I won't be disembodied spirits hovering in an ethereal world. We will get to experience every sight, sound, taste, and smell as we physically experience Jesus Christ's reign on this earth. Close your eyes and try to picture walking up the marble steps of a grand building, entering a vast hall, and seeing at its end your Savior sitting on His throne. Wow, what a moment that will be when it happens!

During the millennium, there will be peace on earth. All God's creatures will dwell together in harmony. The Lord Himself will be among His people, and they will worship Him in person. And in some capacity or other, we, the resurrected, will have authority and leadership as Christ's representatives.

What an exciting time that will be![6]

1. What will the earth be like during the millennium after all the destruction of the tribulation has taken place?

Amir: According to Zechariah 14, when Jesus' feet touch down on the Mount of Olives at His return, living waters will begin to flow from Jerusalem, bringing life to the Dead Sea and the rest of the world. Zechariah said this will happen during both summer and winter, which means it will affect both hemispheres simultaneously, bringing life back to the seas and restoring Eden-like conditions to the earth (verses 7-12).

When the second bowl judgment takes place during the tribulation, every living creature in the sea will die and the oceans will become "blood as of a dead man" (Revelation 16:3). Like Zechariah, the prophet Ezekiel spoke of this time of physical restoration that will flow from Jerusalem. In chapter 47, he wrote that wherever the waters flow from the threshold of the temple, there will be healing and life. The Dead Sea will be brought back to life, and fishermen will stand on its shores again, able to catch the same kind of fish found in "the Great Sea," or the Mediterranean (verses 9-10). Ezekiel 47 also says that the waters from the Temple Mount will nourish the trees along the banks of the river, and they will bear fruit every month of the year (verse 12).

All of this tells us that when Jesus comes back, He will bring healing to a devastated earth.

Barry: Isaiah 11 paints a wonderful picture of what I like to call the restoration of an Eden-like condition to the earth. There, the prophet wrote of a time when "the wolf...shall dwell with the lamb, the leopard shall lie down with the young goat, the calf and the young lion and the fatling together; and a child shall lead them" (verse 6). The animals who once preyed on others will be friends, and the animosity between man and the animal kingdom will be restored to what it was in Eden. "The lion shall eat straw like the ox. The nursing child shall play by the cobra's hole, and the weaned child shall put his hand in the viper's den" (verses 7-8). Isaiah 65:20 further tells us that when someone dies at 100 years old, it will be as though a child had died. Humans will once again enjoy a longer lifespan, as happened in Noah's day, when people lived for hundreds of years.

People often ask: What is the purpose of the millennium? I can offer only an opinion. Consider this: Things got pretty messed up on earth even when there were only two people on the planet, and since then, the earth has never been run and experienced the way it should be. In the beginning, Adam and Eve walked in the cool of the day in the garden with the Lord. During the millennium, Jesus will be seated on David's throne ruling in righteousness. While sin will still be present in the world, it will be dealt with instantly and righteously. This means that for the first time in human history since the garden of Eden, this planet will be as close as it can be to what God first intended—until the end of the millennium, when God will create a new heaven and earth.

While earth will not be perfect during the millennium, it will be far more wonderful than it ever was since the fall of man, when the ground was cursed and brought forth thorns and thistles. The earth will be an amazing place during the millennium, but there will still be sin, and where there is sin, there will be death.

2. What will believers do during the millennium?

Barry: The short answer is that believers will rule and reign with Christ. I personally believe that the parables of the talents and the minas could be pointing to how God will judge and reward believers in preparation for the millennium.

In Matthew 25:14-30, in the parable of the talents, those who did more with what the Lord gave them received more. Those who did nothing with what they were given had it taken away, and were cast into outer darkness. In Luke 19:11-27, in the parable of the minas, the same kind of scenario is played out. Those who multiplied what was entrusted to them were rewarded, and those who did nothing met the same fate as those who did nothing with the talents they were given. In this case, the faithful were made rulers over cities.

That we will rule and reign with Christ during the millennium is fact. It may be that our level of responsibility, or the number of cities we rule over, will be determined by what we did with what the

Lord entrusted to us before we died or were raptured. This is speculation, to be sure, but it is calculated speculation because we do know that when we stand before the *bema* seat of Christ (2 Corinthians 5:10), we will be rewarded for what we did for His glory and kingdom while on earth (1 Corinthians 3:12-15). Whatever responsibility we are given as we rule with Christ during the millennium, it will be glorious, and we will perform our service as "kings and priests to His God and Father" (Revelation 1:6).

Amir: I have often wondered why we will have to come back to earth after having already been in heaven! The reason is that God's plan for the future includes the earthly rule of Jesus Christ. In Psalm 132:11-12, the Lord promised King David, "I will set upon your throne the fruit of your body...forevermore." We also know from Isaiah 9:6 that someday, the government of the world "will be upon His shoulder"—that is, Christ's shoulder. This tells us that someday, the Messiah must rule on the earth, for David's throne is an earthly throne, not a heavenly one.

We will also be involved in judging the earth—not in the eternal sense, but the temporal. Matters of dispute between the unglorified inhabitants of this planet will be judged by those who have been glorified and returned to earth to rule in righteousness with Christ.

The fact that we will rule and have a judiciary role on earth—along with Jesus—tells us there will be sin, which means unglorified humans will live on the planet during that time. These unglorified people will be born to believers who survive the tribulation and are welcomed into the millennial kingdom. And these offspring, like all humans, will possess the free will to obey or reject the Lord and His commands. Zechariah 14:17-18 says that those who refuse to come up to Jerusalem to keep the Feast of Tabernacles will experience no rain on their land.

The earth will be a very different place during the millennium, both spiritually and physically. Jesus will be in charge, and all judgment will be swift, fair, and righteous. According to Zechariah 14:20-21, the focus of the millennium, on every level of life, will be "holiness to the LORD."

3. When will the dividing of the sheep and the goats— as mentioned by Jesus in the Olivet Discourse—take place?

Amir: This event will take place at the end of the tribulation. The sheep represent believing humans who survived the tribulation, and the goats represent unbelieving humans who survived. The sheep are identified by one specific characteristic: how they treated the brethren of the Lord, meaning the Jews. Those who helped them and showed charity through humanitarian efforts will give evidence that they are sheep, and those who did not will reveal themselves to be goats. Before we assume that this means the sheep and goats' salvation will be determined by works, we need to recognize that as with all other believers, the sheep are saved by grace through faith, and their love and care for the Jews will *result* from their salvation, and not be the cause of it.

A key fact to keep in mind is that the tribulation is the seventieth week of Daniel, and during that time, Satan's primary target will be the Jews (though he will definitely target believing Gentiles as well). Zechariah 12:3 says that Jerusalem will be "a very heavy stone for all peoples," which means antisemitism will take place on an unprecedented scale worldwide, and the Jews will be targeted by the masses. We also know from Zechariah 13:8 that two-thirds of the Jews will die in unbelief during the tribulation. Some will lose their lives through the cataclysmic events that occur as a result of God's wrath, and others will die at the hand of the beast of Revelation 13, who will make a seven-year covenant with Israel but break it at the midpoint (Daniel 9:27).

This should remind us that antisemitism before the tribulation is just as evil and anti-Christ as it is during the tribulation. It is not possible to say you love Jesus, the King of the Jews, yet hate the Jews over whom He is King. Loving Israel is not a prerequisite for salvation, but it is one of the many fruits of salvation. When we are saved, we become a new creation. We turn from darkness to light, we change the direction of our thinking, and we bear the fruit of the Spirit rather than the works of the flesh. That means that someone who is antisemitic can still come to Jesus and be saved. But after Jesus saves them, He is going to change them, and they will love Israel because He does.

Barry: In Daniel 12:11-12, Daniel mentions two time periods that seem to be out of sync with other passages related to the tribulation. The terms that are commonly associated with the duration of the tribulation are a time, times, and half a time; 42 months; and 1,260 days. All three spans of time are identical; the tribulation consists of two three-and-a-half-year periods. But Daniel 12:11-12 mentions a span of 1,290 days, and says that those who make it to day 1,335 will be blessed.

These two time periods—1,290 days and 1,335 days—do not contradict the other time spans associated with the tribulation. Rather, they just add further information. Daniel 12:11 says that there are 1,290 days from the time the daily sacrifice is taken away until the end of the tribulation. That means that 30 days prior to the midpoint of the tribulation, the first beast of Revelation 13 will take away the Jews' ability to offer sacrifices—an activity that he initially allowed under the seven-year covenant he made with Daniel's people and the holy city (Daniel 9:24-27). Thirty days later, at the 1,260-day mark, the beast will commit the abomination of desolation by standing in the most holy place and declaring to the world that He is God. This explains the 1,290-day mark: 30 days before the midpoint of the tribulation, the Jews' right to offer sacrifices to God will be taken away. And 30 days later, the abomination of desolation will take place.

But, what about the 1,335 days? You'll notice that 1,335 days brings us to 75 days over and above the 1,260 days of one-half of the tribulation. It seems clear that this extra 75-day period will occur *after* the second coming of Jesus, and this is when the sheep and the goats will be divided, and the goats will be cast into "the everlasting fire prepared for the devil and his angels" (Matthew 25:41). There is, in contrast, a blessing promised to believers who make it to that day, or the time of Jesus' return. According to Matthew 25:34, they will inherit the earthly kingdom with Jesus. The Bible makes it clear that only believers will enter the millennial kingdom after the sheep and goats are divided. These sheep will not be in a glorified state of immortality; they will still possess their mortal human bodies and will have offspring who are born with a sin nature. That is why Christ will need to rule the nations "with a rod of iron" (Psalm 2:9).

4. What does Isaiah 19:24 mean when it says, "Israel will be one of three with Egypt and Assyria"? When does this happen?

Amir: In Revelation 17:10, Egypt and Assyria are the first two of the six empires mentioned that oppressed Israel. Egypt, when Israel was in its infancy, held the Hebrews as slaves for 430 years (Exodus

12:40), and the Assyrians when Israel was divided into northern and southern kingdoms after King Solomon's death (2 Kings 15:29).

Isaiah 19 highlights another beautiful aspect of the millennial kingdom in that not only will animosity between the human and animal kingdoms be repealed, but so too will the national distresses we read about and experience every day. Ancient enemies like Israel and Egypt and Israel and Assyria will be one in the Lord.

If we add verse 25 to Isaiah 19:24, we can see how clearly this is pictured:

> In that day Israel will be one of three with Egypt and Assyria—a blessing in the midst of the land, whom the LORD of hosts shall bless, saying, "Blessed is Egypt My people, and Assyria the work of My hands, and Israel My inheritance."

The timing of this is undoubtably during the millennium because we know the whole world will be gathered against Jerusalem during the tribulation and the city will be a burdensome stone to all peoples (Zechariah 12:3). This is a wonderful picture of the work of Christ in our hearts as He saves us. He makes even ancient enemies one with Him and they with each other. This will never be clearer than during the millennial reign of Christ on earth when Egypt, Assyria, and Israel are one.

Barry: I agree with Amir that the timing is clearly during the millennium. The two nations made one with Israel are interesting and present something worth considering as to why the Spirit chose them among the six who dominated the world scene throughout Israel's history.

The capital city of Assyria was Nineveh, the city to whom the Lord sent the reluctant prophet Jonah with a very short and distinct message: "Yet forty days, and Nineveh shall be overthrown!" (Jonah 3:4). The response to this short, straight-to-the-point message was stunning:

> The people of Nineveh believed God, proclaimed a fast, and put on sackcloth, from the greatest to the least of them (Jonah 3:5).

> Then God saw their works, that they turned from their evil way; and God relented from the disaster that He had said He would bring upon them, and He did not do it (verse 10).

This "awakening" lasted 100 years. Then after the people had returned to their old ways, the Lord sent the prophet Nahum to Nineveh to repeat Jonah's message to them. The people did not repent, and Nineveh ended up being destroyed.

Alexandria, Egypt, was home to Apollos, who ministered with the great apostle Paul. Apollos was described as "an eloquent man and mighty in the Scriptures" (Acts 18:24). The Septuagint, the Greek translation of the Hebrew Old Testament, began to be produced there, and the Alexandrian text is considered one of the earliest copies of the Greek New Testament. The city was also the home of early church fathers like Clement, Origen, and Athanasius. This tells us the church in Alexandria was strong during the early days of Christianity.

One fact that you will never see in the news is that currently, the church in Egypt is growing very rapidly. There are tens of thousands of house churches springing up, most of which are attended by converts from Islam. The vast majority of Assyrians today live in diaspora scattered around the world, as Israel was for 2,000 years. Yet the Assyrians, like the Israelites, have maintained their national identity, and a major portion of the Assyrian population in Egypt is Christian.

Not to be dogmatic, but could these ancient enemies of Israel become one with the Jewish people during the millennium because of the seeds of the gospel that were sown by the ancestors who put their belief in God? Note what Proverbs 16:7 says: "When a man's ways please the LORD, He makes even his enemies to be at peace with him."

Egypt and Assyria and Israel all coming to know the Lord is how former enemies can become the one people of God. Isaiah 19:24 foretells of just how far the love of God can take people when they, despite their countries' failures, stay true to God and His Word.

5. What is the purpose of sacrifices at the millennial temple if Jesus was the perfect sacrifice?

Barry: The fact there will be sacrifices offered at the millennial temple has confused many. A key verse that can help our understanding of this is Hebrews 10:4, which says, "It is not possible that the blood of bulls and goats could take away sins." The previous verse made the argument that if the blood of the sacrifices could satisfy our sin debt, then why was it necessary for them to be offered over and over, year after year?

The confusion about sacrifices offered in the millennial temple comes from the fact many people don't realize the role of the sacrifices in the first place. They could not take away sin. Rather, the people were to bring sacrifices to the Lord so they would be reminded that innocent blood must be shed for sin. The sacrifices of the Old Testament did not remove anyone's sin. Instead, they pointed to the ultimate sacrifice that would never need to be repeated: The shedding of Christ's blood, which had atoning power for the sins of the whole world (1 John 2:2). The Old Testament sacrifices pointed to Jesus, and the sacrifices offered at the fourth temple—during the millennium—will do the same.

Amir: Ezekiel 45 describes the sacrifices in the millennial temple as sin offerings. The priests are instructed to "take some of the blood of the sin offering and put it on the doorposts of the temple, on the four corners of the ledge of the altar, and on the gateposts of the gate of the inner court. And so you shall do on the seventh day of the month for everyone who has sinned unintentionally or in ignorance. Thus you shall make atonement for the temple" (verses 19-20).

We are also told that people will observe Passover and give grain offerings along with oil (verses 21-24). Passover is the one feast that is mentioned in the instructions for the sacrifices offered during the millennium. Passover observes the time when, in ancient Egypt, the Israelites were commanded to apply the blood of a lamb to the doorposts and lintels of their homes to protect them from the death angel who "passed over" all the homes in Egypt and killed the Egyptian firstborn. The Israelites who had done as they were commanded were protected.

If Hebrews 10:4 says it is impossible for the blood of bulls and goats to take away sins, then that will also be true of the sacrifices offered during the millennium. The sin offerings made under the law pointed forward to the One whose blood would be sufficient to cover man's sins, and the sacrifices made in the millennial temple will point back to Christ's death on the cross as well. They will serve to remind the mortal offspring of those who survived the tribulation that sin is costly, and that only the blood of Jesus can cover their sins.

The shedding of blood is a sacred ceremony, much like the taking of communion is for the church. The communion elements represent something far greater than themselves, as do the sacrifices of the millennium. They point to the blood of Jesus, which protects those who have received Him as their Savior. It is because of Christ's work at the cross that the second death passes over those who are covered by His blood.

6. Why is it necessary for the devil to be released at the end of the millennium?

Barry: The only information Scripture provides for us appears in Revelation 20:8-9. There, we read that he will be released, and he will "go out to deceive the nations which are in the four corners of the earth, Gog and Magog, to gather them together to battle, whose number is as the sand of the sea" (verse 8). Then fire will come down from heaven and devour them (verse 9). Nowhere in that passage do we see God's motivation for releasing Satan.

I believe we can apply some calculated speculation to this passage, but any conclusions we arrive at should not be treated dogmatically. In looking back over history, the release of Satan after 1,000 years of righteous rule over the earth brings the world to a place where it could be said that God has sought to communicate His love and truth to the world through every means possible. He walked with man in the cool of the day in the garden of Eden, and man chose disobedience over fellowship. He gave man a law through Moses as a means by which life could be lived at its best, and man chose disobedience over acceptance. He then sent His only begotten Son into the world in the likeness of sinful human flesh to offer Himself as the perfect sacrifice for the sins of the whole world, and man chose religion over being made righteous. Finally, God will send His Son back into the world not as a Lamb slain, but as the Lion of Judah, to rule and reign in righteousness. And after 1,000 years of the King of kings' rule on earth, Satan will be released, and multitudes numbering like the sand of the sea (Revelation 20:8) will choose to side with Satan against God.

The release of Satan and the defection of the nations to follow him—after all they have seen of Christ's rule for 1,000 years—justifies what happens next in the chronology of history, the Great White Throne judgment. God will have tried to reach man in every way possible with the hope of heaven through His plan of salvation, and yet untold billions will reject His offer of salvation and side with the devil in spite of all that God has communicated to man. This, I believe, could be a possible reason that God will release Satan at the end of the millennium—this will show that God has given man every opportunity, and even then, many will choose sin over salvation.

Amir: One fact we know for sure is that the heart of man is deceitful and desperately wicked (Jeremiah 17:9). That will be evident by the fact so many people choose to follow Satan after he is released. To choose the devil over Jesus—even after all the blessings the earth has experienced under Christ's rule for 1,000 years—shows the hardness of man's heart. To see the King of kings in person, to experience the blessings of His righteousness and His justice, to enjoy earthly life as God had intended in Eden-like conditions, to see the lion and the lamb lie down together, and for people to enjoy such long lives, yet choose to follow Satan, reveals the condition of man's heart.

You may have heard the saying, "The heart of the problem is the problem of the heart." God does everything possible to prove His love, and we have to remember that at the beginning of the millennium, everyone is a believer. The glorified saints will rule with Jesus, there will be no corrupt political system, there will be no famines or catastrophic events, there will be no wars and rumors of wars, and there will be no more elections with politicians who make promises and then break them. The One who is the way, the truth, and the life will be ruling the world. Even in the best environment possible, after Satan is let loose, an army of people numbering like the sand of the sea will choose him over the Prince of Peace and Lord of lords. The desperately wicked state of fallen mankind's heart, apart from God, will be revealed one last time at the end of the millennium.

7. Are the Gog and Magog mentioned in Revelation 20 the same Gog and Magog of Ezekiel chapters 38–39?

Amir: Even though Gog and Magog are mentioned in both Revelation 20 and Ezekiel 38–39, the two passages feature completely different scenes. In Ezekiel 38–39, a coalition of nations will invade Israel, and the ancient names of these nations are listed for us in Ezekiel 38:2-6. In this list, we can identify the modern-day nations of Russia, Turkey, Iran, Libya, and Sudan. They will invade from the north and will be destroyed by God, and it will take seven months to bury the dead after the Lord's decisive victory over Israel's enemies. In Revelation 20:8, where Gog and Magog are mentioned again, 1,000 years will have passed, and this time, the battle won't be against Israel, but against the saints who ruled with Christ during the millennium. And the enemies will come not from a handful of nations, as happens in Ezekiel 38–39, but from the four corners of the earth, and they will number like the sand of the sea.

These differences between the two passages make it clear these are two different battles. Also, after the Ezekiel war, the land will be cleansed and the dead will be buried. But after the war in Revelation 20, the devil and all who followed him will be called to account at the Great White Throne judgment. Then they will be condemned, and join the beast and false prophet in the lake of fire, never to be seen or heard from again.

The two Gog and Magog wars are more than 1,000 years apart, but the enemy behind both is the same: Satan. The question you need to answer for yourself is this: Will you be present for the Revelation 20 war of Gog and Magog? Will you be among those who rule with Jesus from Jerusalem? And be on the right side of the battle? That means choosing to put your belief in Jesus and receiving Him as your Savior and Lord.

Barry: In Genesis 10, which is commonly referred to as the table of nations, we find the descendants of Noah listed by name, and the participants in the Ezekiel invasion are included there under their ancient names. Thus, the modern geographic regions they represent can be determined by tracing where the descendants of Noah settled. The one name in Ezekiel 38:2-6 that is not found in the table of nations is Gog. Some Bible commentators have proposed that this could indicate that Gog is a fallen angel assigned to the nation of Israel, much like the Lord had assigned Michael the position of chief prince over Israel.

Daniel 10:13 mentions that there was a prince of the kingdom of Persia who was hindering the delivery of an answer to Daniel's prayer, until Michael was dispatched from heaven to deal with him. Some have proposed that Gog is the name or title of the fallen angel assigned to harass and destroy Israel, which would make it possible for it to be present at two wars 1,000 years apart. Whether that is true or not remains to be seen, but what we do know for sure is that the combatants listed in Ezekiel 38–39 are different from those in

Revelation 20. The theaters of engagement are different as well, and both battles have distinctly different outcomes. This means they are not the same event, even though Gog and Magog are mentioned in both passages.

Whether Gog is a fallen angel assigned by the devil to harass the chosen people, or Gog is figurative of the earthly enemies of God, what we do know with certainty is that the war in Revelation 20 will end with Satan being cast into hell forever and ever. At this time, the Great White Throne judgment will take place, and for everyone who is present at that judgment, it will be too late to repent. Their eternal destiny will have already been sealed. They will be sentenced according to every violation of God's law and their rejection of God's offer of forgiveness through Christ—and their condemnation will be just.

THE GREAT WHITE THRONE JUDGMENT

THE GREAT WHITE THRONE JUDGMENT

n Revelation 20:12, after the end of the millennium, John the Revelator describes for us what will take place in heaven:

> I saw the dead, small and great, standing before God, and books were opened. And another book was opened, which is the Book of Life. And the dead were judged according to their works, by the things which were written in the books.

Imagine this amazing scene: Countless people will be standing before God. The books will be opened, and one by one, men and women from all generations will be judged based on their actions during their lives. Daniel is even more picturesque in his description of this same courtroom:

> I watched till thrones were put in place,
> and the Ancient of Days was seated;
> His garment was white as snow,
> and the hair of His head was like pure wool.
> His throne was a fiery flame,
> its wheels a burning fire;
> a fiery stream issued
> and came forth from before Him.
> A thousand thousands ministered to Him;
> ten thousand times ten thousand stood before Him.
> The court was seated,
> and the books were opened (Daniel 7:9-10).

Known as the Great White Throne judgment, this will be a public trial. With God, the sins of every person there will be in the open. There will be nothing left hidden. Every action with its shame and guilt will be laid bare. Then will come the verdict: "Guilty!" This is a scene that should make us shudder and be filled with sorrow. However, for those of us who are believers, it should not fill us with fear because we will not be judged in this courtroom. We will be in the gallery as observers, not before the throne as defendants.[7]

1. What is the difference between the first and second resurrections?

Barry: We can understand the distinction between the two resurrections by recognizing that the first one is a "category" and not an event. Revelation 20:6 says that "the second death has no power" over those who take part in the first resurrection. Two verses earlier, we read that those who were beheaded "for their witness to Jesus and the word of God" will be part of the first resurrection. They will have been beheaded because they refused to accept the mark of the beast. We also know that at the second coming of Jesus, when the Jews alive at the time recognize Jesus as the Holy One of Israel, their Savior, the Old Testament saints who believed God will be physically resurrected as well.

The first resurrection is a category of people over whom the second death has no power because they believed God, and this will be accounted to them as righteousness. Old Testament saints who believed the Messiah was coming through the line of Judah, New Testament saints who believed Jesus of Nazareth was the long-awaited Savior, tribulation saints who had the same testimony, and believers in Christ as Savior and Lord during the millennium will all participate in the first resurrection, even though their bodily resurrections will occur at different times.

The second resurrection, however, is both an event and a category. This resurrection will take place at the end of the millennium (Revelation 20:5), when all the unbelieving dead from history are bodily raised to stand before God and, as a category, collectively represent all peoples from every age of history who have rejected God for whatever reason. They will stand before God as He sits on His throne and bow and confess that Jesus is Lord, but theirs will not be a confession that leads to forgiveness and thus salvation. The Bible absolutely refutes any after-death opportunities for a person to be saved, and does not teach the idea that we can go to a place of suffering to be purged of our sin. Hebrews 9:27 clearly says, "It is appointed for men to die once, but after this the judgment."

Amir: You don't want to be part of the second resurrection. You don't want to be among those who, at that time, will make the forced confession that Jesus is Lord and bow the knee to Him. You want to be part of the first resurrection, which encompasses all believers from every age. You want to be part of those who confess *now* that Jesus is Lord—not later at the Great White Throne judgment, for then it will be too late.

Included among the people who are part of the second resurrection will be those who thought good moral behavior or religious observance could save them. This group will include people who thought being born part of a certain group could save them. Just because you have the word "Christian" printed on your birth certificate doesn't mean you are saved. This group will also include those who said in their hearts, "There is no God." Their names will not be written in the Lamb's Book of Life.

The first resurrection is comprised of people who meet one qualification: Their names are written in the Book of Life. Some people say that all names are written in the Book of Life, and then some are blotted out through unbelief. Others say names are written into the Book of Life through belief in Jesus Christ. Whatever the case may be, the only names that will appear in the Book of Life are those of people who have believed and trusted in God's only plan of salvation though Jesus Christ. Whether they were an Old Testament saint looking forward to the cross or a New Testament saint looking back at the cross, the blood of Jesus is what keeps or puts our names into the Book of Life.

The second resurrection will involve those who are judged by two books—one that lists all their works throughout life, good and bad, and the fact their names do not appear in the Book of Life. Revelation 20:13 says each person at the second resurrection will be judged "according to his works." As we know, good works cannot save a person's soul. Our eternal destination will not be determined by weighing our good works against our bad. No amount of works can achieve salvation. A person must place their faith in Christ alone to be saved. And if a person's name is not found in the Lamb's Book of Life, he or she will be cast into the lake of fire, which is hell.

2. What does it mean that death and Hades are cast into the lake of fire?

Amir: The Great White Throne judgment is the final event before eternity begins for all unbelieving humans who have ever lived. Revelation 20:13 tells us what will happen: "The sea gave up the dead who were in it, and Death and Hades delivered up the dead who were in them." This is the second resurrection, or the bodily resurrection of the unbelieving dead. Death—meaning the grave—will be destroyed, and the temporary domain of the unbelieving dead, Hades, will no longer be needed. They will both be cast into the lake of fire, which is the second death and therefore, hell. Death and Hades are holding places for people until the second resurrection takes place.

After the millennium, the saints of all the ages will live forever in an immortal and incorruptible state. There will be no more death for them. And the lake of fire will be the eternal home for those who rejected Christ as Savior and Lord. Sadly, many people today overlook the fact that everyone will live forever, but not in the same place. Some people teach that after death, it's possible for people to go through a purification process in a place called purgatory. They say that after a person's sins have been purged or penance is paid, then he or she can spend eternity in heaven. And there are others who say that everyone will go to heaven because God is love, and love doesn't judge and send people to a place like hell.

Neither of those teachings are biblical. You cannot be purged of your sins and saved after you die. And not everyone goes to heaven, even though God is love. Someday, death will be cast into hell with Hades, which means eternal life in the lake of fire will be the inescapable destiny of all unbelievers.

Barry: "Anyone not found written in the Book of Life was cast into the lake of fire" (Revelation 20:15) is one of the most chilling statements in all of literature. In the very next verse, in Revelation 21, we read that a new heaven and new earth will be created, and the old heaven and earth will pass away. We can conclude that the new heaven and new earth will be the dwelling places of all who became new creations in Christ during their lifetime, and that the lake of fire will be the eternal destiny of those who did not.

Some dare to say that eternity in hell is a disproportionate response to human sin. It's arrogant to make such a statement, for it means that humans know better than God how to exercise justice. The truth is that hell is the choice of all who go there. First John 2:2 says Jesus died for the sins of the whole world, yet John 1:12 reminds us that only those who have received Him—those who believe His name—are given "the right to become children of God."

You cannot accuse God of unfairness nor a disproportionate response to human sin when it was His own Son who shed His blood to redeem us and cover our sins.

3. Can a Christian have their name blotted out from the Book of Life and end up at the Great White Throne judgment?

Barry: In Revelation 3:5, Jesus said, "He who overcomes shall be clothed in white garments, and I will not blot out his name from the Book of Life." Some take this to mean that it is possible for someone to be saved and then lose their salvation, resulting in their name being blotted out of the Book of Life. And the apostle John spoke of those who "went out from us, but they were not of us" (1 John 2:19). He said that those who depart from the faith were never of the faith in the first place. And in the Sermon on the Mount, Jesus said there will be those who claim to have done many things in His name, yet He never knew them because they practiced lawlessness (Matthew 7:21-23).

It is helpful for us to look at Jesus' words in Revelation 3:5 as a promise and not a threat. Let's look carefully at what He said: "He who overcomes…I will not blot out his name from of the Book of Life." This implies *not* that those who overcome can be blotted out, but rather, that those who do not overcome will be blotted out.

In addition, Romans 8:1 promises that there is no condemnation to those who are in Christ Jesus. For these reasons, I do not believe that a person who has been saved can lose their salvation and wind up at the Great White Throne judgment to be condemned to hell.

Amir: No, we cannot lose our salvation! We are new creations in Christ, and nowhere does the Bible teach that you can un-become a new creation. If old things have passed away and all things have become new (1 Corinthians 5:17), those new things cannot become old again.

According to Ephesians 1:13, after we trust in Jesus, we are "sealed with the Holy Spirit of promise," which guarantees our future inheritance. First Peter 1:3-5 says that those who have been begotten again (born again) "to a living hope through the resurrection of Jesus Christ" have "an inheritance incorruptible and undefiled…reserved in heaven." And we're told that we "are kept by the power of God through faith for salvation."

If you have been born again, you have a place reserved for you in heaven. Your reservation cannot be canceled, nor can your name be blotted out from the Book of Life. Now, as indicated by what Jesus said in Matthew 7:21-23, it's possible for people to think their name is written in the Book of Life when it is not. How can we know for sure that we are in the Book of Life? In 2 Corinthians 13:5, Paul urged, "Examine yourselves as to whether you are in the faith. Test yourselves." How do you test yourself? Paul says to make sure "Jesus Christ is in you." If you don't believe the Bible, if you reject parts of the Bible, if you think you can get to heaven through good works, if you think there is no hell and all judgment is wrong, Christ is not in you because Jesus is the Word of God. When Christ is truly in you, you will never deny the hard truths of the Bible, even when they're difficult to understand.

Born-again, Spirit-filled, Bible-believing Christians—which are the only kind of Christian there is—will not have their name blotted out from the Book of Life. They will not wind up at the Great White Throne judgment.

4. Are those who are destined for the lake of fire consumed, or do they exist there forever?

Amir: The doctrine of annihilationism is not biblical. This is the belief that those who are cast into the lake of fire, or hell, will be consumed by the flames and cease to exist. This is easily disproven through what happens to the unholy trinity of the beast, false prophet, and Satan himself. Revelation 19:20 says that the beast and the false prophet will be captured and cast alive into the lake of fire. And Revelation 20:10 says that 1,000 years later, at the end of the millennium, Satan will be thrown into the lake of fire, where the beast and false prophet are—"and they will be tormented day and night forever and ever."

When Satan, a fallen angel, is cast into the lake of fire, the beast and false prophet, who are both human beings, will have already been there for 1,000 years. This tells us people who go to hell will not be consumed and cease to exist. Rather, hell is a place of eternal torment. There is nothing temporary about it, nor does the Bible ever imply that the unbelieving dead will eventually cease to exist.

In Mark 9:44, Jesus described hell as a place where "their worm does not die and the fire is not quenched." The worms He spoke of are maggots that feed on dead things, and figuratively, they represent internal torment, whereas the fire refers to external torment. Jesus' words state very clearly this is a place of ongoing and unending punishment. The bodies and souls that go to hell will not be consumed and cease to exist.

Barry: I believe the reason so many people are hesitant to accept the fact that hell is a real place of eternal punishment is twofold: People have not fully grasped the gravity of sin and the holiness of God. In Romans 5:12, Paul wrote, "Through one man sin entered the world, and death through sin." We need to recognize that sin has killed every human ever born, with the exceptions of Enoch, Elijah, and those living believers who will be raptured. We also need to grasp just how holy God is. Interestingly, there are only two times that the Bible says God is love, but some 400 times that it says God is holy.

Sin is so offensive to God and so costly to humanity that it required the blood of God's own Son to cover it so that man could be reconciled to God. Hell is hardly a disproportionate response to sin in light of the gravity of sin and the holiness of God. Throughout the Old Testament, man killed God's prophets, then when Jesus came, man killed Him too. We've also seen how, through the ages, people have tried to eliminate God's chosen people. And during the tribulation, they will reject God even though they realize the wrath they are experiencing is a result of their rebellion.

Hell might be an uncomfortable reality for us to consider, but our discomfort with the fact of hell should never lead to our minimizing the reality of it. Hell is a place of eternal torment for the unbelieving dead, not a fire that consumes their bodies and souls so that they cease to exist. The biblical evidence, the gravity of sin, and the holiness of God all bear witness against the doctrine of annihilationism.

CHAPTER 7

HEAVEN

HEAVEN

What will heaven be like? The Bible gives us some details, but there is much we aren't told about.

After the millennium is over and the Great White Throne judgment has taken place, the apostle John pulls back the curtain and unveils the future new heaven and new earth:

> Now I saw a new heaven and a new earth, for the first heaven and the first earth had passed away. Also there was no more sea. Then I, John, saw the holy city, New Jerusalem, coming down out of heaven from God, prepared as a bride adorned for her husband (Revelation 21:1-2).

A new beginning—how wonderful! Sometimes something is just so far gone that there is nothing left to do except start over. In

Greek, there are two words that can be translated "new." One is *chronos*, which primarily refers to something that is "new in time." You used to drive an old car, but now you drive a new car. The second word is *kainos*, and it means "new in kind." This is what we find John using in this passage.

The new heaven and the new earth will not only be new, but, more importantly, they will be superior in quality to the old. The new will never perish, as did the old ones. This new creation will not be infected by sin, nor will it ever be. Death will never be seen in God's upgraded handiwork. When the old goes and the new comes, everything will be made better.

As for the New Jerusalem—it will be massive! It's not normal city big or even country big. It's continent big. It's wider than Europe from London to Kiev. Whatever mountaintop John was standing on, the New Jerusalem had to have some serious elevation for him to be able to see more than just one small portion of one enormous wall. And, oh, is it beautiful! Like the most perfect of gemstones are its walls and its foundations and its gates and its streets.

Through the rest of Revelation 21, John presents a description of the New Jerusalem and says it is dressed as a beautiful bride would be for her husband. Why does God provide these details? Maybe because He wants to create within us a bit of anticipation for our future home. If He gives too much detail, our focus might excessively shift to the future and we will be of no use serving Him today. If He gives too little detail, there will be no anticipation. So like a parent who covers a Christmas gift with festive paper and elaborate bows to excite the imagination of a child, God presents us with just enough of a picture to stir our anticipation and build our expectations.[8]

1. Are the mansions that Jesus is preparing for us part of the city that will come down from heaven in the future?

Amir: No, our heavenly mansions are not part of the New Jerusalem. We know that because Jesus said He is coming to take us to be where He is, in His Father's house. This is where we will be during the tribulation—in places prepared for us in heaven. The new heavens and earth will not have been created yet. We will be taken up to the old heaven, which is beautiful in its glory and splendor, as revealed in Revelation 4. But we have to remember that Satan will have access to heaven until he is thrown down from his former ability to access the throne room of God and comes to the earth knowing he has but a short time, as Revelation 12 says. The new Jerusalem will be a place in which righteousness dwells, and according to Revelation 21:27, nothing will be allowed to enter that "causes an abomination or a lie." Satan, being the father of lies (John 8:44), will never enter the New Jerusalem.

Also, after Jesus takes us up to the Father's house to be with Him, we will be there for only seven years. Then we will return to the earth for 1,000 years to rule with Him. After that will come the Great White Throne judgment, after which the old heavens and earth will pass away and be replaced by a new heavens and earth.

After the rapture, we will live in the heavenly mansions for only a short time, yet Jesus has been preparing these places for us for 2,000 years. They will be amazing and beautiful, but they are not the New Jerusalem.

Barry: I love what Paul said in 2 Corinthians 12, where he talked about the time he was caught up into heaven and heard inexpressible things that were not lawful for a man to utter (verses 2-4). If we pair this with the description John gave of God's throne room in Revelation 4, we can conclude that the place Jesus will take us to after the rapture is unbelievably beautiful and majestic.

When I talk to people about Revelation 4, I enjoy pointing out that someday, we are going to see all that is described there. Imagine hearing the voices of the four living creatures who never rest day and night, saying, "Holy, holy, holy, Lord God Almighty, who was and is and is to come!" (verse 8). Add to that the 24 elders seated on thrones around the throne of the all-powerful King of heaven. We are going to see the emerald-colored circular rainbow around God's throne and the crystal sea in front of His throne. We're going to see the 24 elders fall down before Him who sits on the throne in response to the proclamation of the four living creatures and add to their own proclamation: "You are worthy, O Lord, to receive glory and honor and power; for You created all things, and by Your will they exist and were created" (verse 11). Even though we will be there for only seven years, it will be a truly glorious seven years!

I always find it curious that there are those who like to point out that the Greek word translated "mansions" can be translated "dwelling places." This seems to be an effort to downplay that there will be mansions in heaven awaiting us. We need to remember and rejoice in the fact that heaven is nothing like earth. What would you expect to live in when you get to heaven—the projects? Why diminish the words of Jesus when everything else we read about heaven is beyond our imagination or description?

That which awaits us after the rapture is unbelievable. And after the millennium, everything will get even better. We will live in new heavens and a new earth, along with a New Jerusalem that is so beautiful that John describes it as being like a bride on her wedding day (Revelation 21:2). In the Father's house are many mansions, and Jesus is preparing one of them for me—and one for you!

2. Are there different levels of heaven?

Barry: In 2 Corinthians 12:2, Paul wrote about being "caught up to the third heaven." This third heaven is the domain of the angels and the throne room of God. The second heaven is the heavens where the stars dwell, and the first heaven is the realm where the birds fly. When Paul spoke about the third heaven, he wasn't saying there are three levels of the highest heaven itself, where God dwells.

Scripture teaches that believers will receive levels of rewards in heaven, but this does not mean there are different levels of heaven itself. There will be one New Jerusalem, and that will be the domain of all believers from every age of history. Yes, there will be rewards after our works are tested by fire (1 Corinthians 3:13-14). Depending on the outcome of that test by fire, some will receive more rewards than others. But this doesn't mean some believers will have access to certain parts of heaven that others won't have. We will all dwell in the same place, and we will be like Jesus. We will not have any pride over our own accomplishments, we will rejoice in what others have done, and there will be no jealousy or competitive spirit among us. This is all part of what makes heaven *heaven*.

Amir: The New Jerusalem described in Revelation 21 has specific dimensions. We're told that the length, breadth, and height are all the same: 12,000 furlongs, or around 1,500 miles. Some believe this city will be a cube; others say it will have a pyramid shape. The massive height seems to imply many levels, or floors, but they will all be part of just one city. There is nothing that indicates certain areas will be exclusive to a particular group of believers, which is really the heart of the question above. There is no evidence that some residents will live at a higher level of heaven than others. Revelation 21:3 indicates that *all* those who are saved will enter the city and be in God's presence.

The New Testament also teaches about five different heavenly crowns that will be received by believers: the imperishable crown (1 Corinthians 9:24-27), the crown of rejoicing (1 Thessalonians 2:19), the crown of righteousness (1 Timothy 4:7-8), the crown of glory (1 Peter 5:1-4), and the crown of life (James 1:12).

Yet the crowns and rewards should not be taken to mean we will be placed in or given access to some parts of heaven and not others. Everyone will share the same access to the New Jerusalem.

3. Will we be the same person in heaven that we were on earth?

Amir: I believe the answer can be found though the story of Jesus' transfiguration, which is recorded in Matthew, Mark, and Luke. When Jesus was transfigured, two long-gone Old Testament saints appeared and talked with Him: Moses and Elijah, representing the law and the prophets. They weren't a different Moses and Elijah; they were the Moses and Elijah of the Bible. Peter knew who they were, likely because Jesus introduced them, but the point is that even after Moses and Elijah were on the other side of death, they were the same persons that they were when they lived on earth.

Also, when we stand at the *bema* seat, or Christ's judgment seat (2 Corinthians 5:10), our works will be judged for both what we did and why we did them during life on earth. This tells us that our identity on earth will clearly be our identity in heaven.

Barry: In Philippians 3:20-21, Paul wrote that our citizenship is in heaven and that our lowly bodies will be upgraded to an eternal and glorious body conformed into the image of Christ. Paul made a similar statement in 1 Corinthians 15:53, saying that our mortal, corruptible bodies will be made into immortal, incorruptible bodies. This implies that our identity will travel with us from here to eternity.

Also, after Jesus rose again and met Mary at the garden tomb, note that she called Him "Rabboni!" (John 20:16). Even in His glorified body, she knew who He was. When the post-resurrection Jesus met the disciples at the Sea of Galilee for breakfast, we're told they dared not ask who He was because they knew it was the Lord (John 21:12). After Jesus rose from the dead, He was recognized by those who knew Him. This assures us that we will be known in heaven as we were known on earth, even though we will be a glorified and perfected version of our former selves.

4. Will we be aware of those we knew or loved who did not go to heaven?

Barry: There are people who ask, "How can heaven be heaven when people whom we knew and loved ended up going to hell?" There are two possible answers to this. First, when Revelation 21:4 says that God will wipe away every tear from our eyes, it's possible that He will erase our memory of those who didn't end up in heaven. Second, 1 John 3:2 says that when we see Jesus, we will be like Him. This means we will see everything from His perspective, and we will see hell as a just and fair punishment for those who rejected God's offer of salvation.

There may be other possibilities, but those seem like the most plausible, given the limited knowledge that we have. It helps to remember that we are going to a place that is beyond what we are able to imagine. If Paul said he heard things so incredible they were unlawful to utter, imagine what he saw (2 Corinthians 12:2-4)! First Corinthians 2:9 says, "Eye has not seen, nor ear heard…the things which God has prepared for those who love Him." Whatever happens regarding our memories that allows "heaven to be heaven," it will not diminish in any way where we are and who we are with. In that day, we will finally be with Jesus.

Amir: I once met a man whose business was flourishing so much that he had bought new cars and was having a magnificent custom home built. He told me he hoped Jesus wasn't coming back too soon because he wanted to enjoy his earthly success for a while. What a wrong perspective to have! Nothing in heaven is going to be lesser than what is on earth. Nothing could be made better; nothing could be improved upon. There are some people who wonder if their pets will be in heaven, and though we do not know the answer, the fact is, having or not having our former pets there will not make heaven any better or worse.

The splendor of heaven will be so great that we will walk on streets of gold (Revelation 21:21), and the city we live in will not need the sun or moon because the Lamb will be its light (verse 23). When you get to heaven, you won't wish you had visited such and such a place on earth before you arrived in heaven. You won't be saying, "I wish I would have had a boyfriend or girlfriend or gotten married or bought my dream car." You won't be thinking about things you wish you had experienced. Rather, all of us will be excited that we are in heaven!

Will we remember the people we knew who have perished and been cast into the lake of fire? The Bible does not say, so we cannot know for sure. What *is* clear is that heaven will be heaven because we will be with the Maker of heaven and earth. No one will go to heaven and wish things were a little bit better by adding this or that.

CHAPTER 8

ADDITIONAL PRESSING QUESTIONS FOR TODAY

ADDITIONAL PRESSING QUESTIONS FOR TODAY

History is moving forward, and the events that are rapidly approaching can be separated into two categories: those we can do something about, and those we can't. Most future happenings fall into the latter category. When the angel Gabriel came to the prophet Daniel, he told him what was going to happen. He said, "Seventy weeks are determined for your people and for your holy city" (Daniel 9:24). The events that Gabriel spoke of *will* take place—they've been determined. You can try to stop the works of God, but you won't get very far. Imagine a speeding train hurtling in your direction. It doesn't matter how earnestly you desire to stop it, that's not going to happen.

If the world's future is so much out of our control, does that mean we are utterly doomed? Is there anything we can do to give ourselves hope in God's grand plan? Most certainly. We can choose to follow Christ, giving ourselves to Him as our Lord and Savior. If we do that, then we are assured that when He returns for His church, we will be taken to Him.

However, if we choose to reject Him—or even if we simply ignore the choice, which is the same as turning our backs on Him—we will be left to experience the terrors of judgment. What a simple choice! Either we choose life eternal or we choose death. Either we choose to escape the wrath of God, or we choose to experience the tribulation and suffer for all eternity apart from our Creator. There is no other decision that we can make in our life that presents such a stark contrast. Praise the Lord that He has given us the opportunity to choose Him! But the day of choosing is now.

Why must it be now? Because the time left for making a choice may soon come to an end. As we keep our eyes on the news, it seems more and more as if the final days are nearly at hand. The news is bleak and the world is on a downward slide. But the Bible says that when you begin to see these things take place, don't let your head droop down in sorrow. Instead, look up—your redemption is drawing near (Luke 21:28). Does that excite you? It should. Jesus is returning for His church, and we could meet Him in the clouds any day now.[9]

1. What about those who say the book of Revelation is allegorical or has already been fulfilled?

Amir: There are many problems with the perspectives that Revelation is to be understood allegorically or historically. A very big one is that the book introduces itself as prophecy (Revelation 1:3), and concludes by saying that it is prophetic (Revelation 22:18).

Those who say that it was prophetic when it was written but is now history have another major problem: None of the prophetic books that talk about the last days have been completely fulfilled yet. For example, Ezekiel 38–39 hasn't happened, Ezekiel 40–48 hasn't happened, Isaiah 60–66 hasn't happened, and Zechariah 12–14 hasn't happened, and they all mention events written about in the book of Revelation.

In response to those who say the book of Revelation is allegorical or figurative, I have to ask: What is the figurative meaning of the four horsemen of the apocalypse in Revelation 6:1-8? Or what is the figurative meaning of the 144,000 virgin, male Jews who are sealed during the tribulation (Revelation 7:2-8)? What is the object lesson of the great mountain burning with fire that is thrown into the sea, or the star Wormwood that poisons a third of the earth's fresh water? What are the locust-like creatures who will ascend from the bottomless pit symbolic of? What is the figurative meaning of Revelation 9:5, which says of these locusts, "They were not given authority to kill them, but to torment them for five months. Their torment was like the torment of a scorpion when it strikes a man"? The problem with saying that Revelation is allegorical is that people can assign any meaning they want to these passages and many others. And there would be no way of knowing who is right or wrong.

Revelation is prophecy, not history or allegory. There are too many parallels in other books like Daniel that have no historical association or allegorical meaning for that to be possible.

Barry: The preterist and partial preterist views that all prophecy is now history—with the exception of the second coming—has an element within them that welcomes a dangerous interpretation of Scripture. That element is Replacement Theology, which teaches that God's unfulfilled promises to Israel now apply to the church. Nothing could be further from the truth!

If the church has replaced Israel in God's plan, why is Ezekiel 37 being fulfilled right before our eyes? Why is the once-barren and forsaken desert now blooming like a rose (Isaiah 35:1)? If the church has replaced Israel and all God's unfulfilled promises now apply to Christians, when did those in the church come up from their graves (Ezekiel 37:12)? What does it mean to those in the church that God will bring them into the land of Israel when believers have been told they are citizens of heaven?

Why are the nations spoken of in Ezekiel 38–39 now actively aligning themselves together and physically placing their armies in the very position God said He would draw them to if this is related to the church? Ezekiel makes it clear this military coalition will invade Israel, not the church. And what about Zechariah 14:2, where God said, "I will gather all the nations to battle against Jerusalem; the city shall be taken, the houses rifled, and the women ravished. Half of the city shall go into captivity, but the remnant of the people shall not be cut off from the city"? That clearly speaks about armies coming against Jerusalem, not the church.

If the promised blessings of Israel now apply to the church, what about the unfulfilled curses and punishments? If they don't apply to the church, why are they in the Bible? Are they wasted words? Are they going to be left unfulfilled? If they are, then that means the Bible is wrong—which is catastrophic!

It is not possible for all the prophecies in Revelation and other parallel passages of Scripture to have been fulfilled in AD 70. Nor does it make sense for all these prophecies to be allegorical. And it is definitely not possible for the Bible's prophecies pertaining to the future of Israel to now apply to the church, for many reasons. One of the most important is that the church does not have a national homeland, but rather, is comprised of people from every tribe, tongue, and nation. God's unfulfilled promises to Israel clearly speak of a return to a homeland, and we have seen that happen over the past century.

The only way the prophetic books make sense is when we interpret them literally from the futurist point of view. Isaiah 7:14 was fulfilled literally; Micah 5:2 was fulfilled literally; Isaiah 53 was fulfilled literally; Acts 1:8 was fulfilled literally; 2 Timothy 3:1-5 is being fulfilled literally right before our eyes; 2 Timothy 4:3-5 is being fulfilled literally right now.

Israel is Israel and the church is the church, and the two are not interchangeable, nor can one replace the other. The only time a scripture written to Israel can be applied to the church is when it concerns God's nature and character because He does not change. God is faithful to Israel, and God is faithful to the church. Jesus is the Holy One and Savior of Israel, and Jesus is the Savior and head of the church.

What would I say to those who teach that all prophecies have already been fulfilled? Just one thing: Why are we seeing prophecies be fulfilled now, right before our eyes, exactly as Scripture said they would be?

2. When will the prophecy in Isaiah 17:1 be fulfilled?

Barry: Based on what we just learned in the previous question, we can say Isaiah 17:1 has not been fulfilled yet. Some suggest that it came to pass under the Assyrian king Sennacherib during the seventh century BC. But that's not possible because Damascus is still a city today. In fact, it boasts of being the world's oldest continuously inhabited city, claiming an uninterrupted history of some 4,500 years. Isaiah 17:1 talks about a day when "Damascus will cease from being a city, and it will become a ruinous heap." That has not happened yet, so this prophecy has yet to be fulfilled.

What country is in the news daily and has been for more than ten years? Syria. What is the inhabited capital of Syria today? Damascus. I believe the fact that Russian, Turkish, and Iranian forces being present inside Syria means that the prophecy in Isaiah 17:1 could potentially be the next one to be fulfilled in the chronology of last-days events. This prophecy is to be understood literally, and we know it has not yet come to pass because Damascus still exists. The city does seem to be in the crosshairs of "soon-to-be-fulfilled prophecies" at this present time.

Amir: I believe that Isaiah 17:1 and Ezekiel 38–39 are companion passages. One leads to the other or even causes the other to happen. You might say that Isaiah 17:1 is the fuse that will ignite the Ezekiel 38–39 war.

Syria is not mentioned among the invading forces in Ezekiel 38:2-6, yet Syria shares a border with Israel and even disputes Israel's right to any of the Golan Heights. Interestingly, Russia agrees with Syria on this point. Syria has been a participant in all the previous major wars against Israel, and yet as far as we can tell, it will not be involved in the biggest one that is yet to come. Why? Damascus will have become a ruinous heap. It seems likely that the destruction of Damascus will embolden the invading forces from the north and bring them down into northern Israel, where they will meet their demise.

Ezekiel 39 says that the forces that invade Israel will be defeated just as they were in 1948, 1967, and 1973. Only this time, they will be destroyed directly by God Himself. He will use an earthquake, flooding rain, and great hailstones, fire, and brimstone (Ezekiel

38:19-23). He will also cause the enemy troops to turn on each other (verse 21), and He will send fire on the land of Magog and those who dwell in the coastlands (Ezekiel 39:6). God will do all this for this reason: "Then the nations shall know that I am the LORD, the Holy One in Israel" (Ezekiel 39:7).

The destruction of Damascus—as prophesied in Isaiah 17:1— will light the fuse to what many call the Middle East powder keg, and that will set a series of prophetic events into motion.

3. Is the United States mentioned in Bible prophecy?

Amir: I do not believe so. The Bible does not state anything about the United States, which makes it reasonable to conclude that in the last days, other nations will rise to power, like Russia and China, and replace the US as the world's superpower. This will likely result from a weakened US government and internal problems that lead other nations to lose their respect for the US. We are already seeing this happen—bully nations like Russia and China no longer show evidence of being intimidated by the US militarily or economically. In the summer of 2021, the surrender of Afghanistan over to the Taliban and the abandonment of America's own citizens when American troops withdrew sent a message to world leaders that the United States has lost its way.

Will America be conquered? Maybe. Will it implode like the Roman Empire? Maybe. We don't know what will happen. But it's telling that when the Ezekiel 38 invasion against Israel takes place, no one will come to Israel's side to help fight their enemies. This seems to indicate that the US either won't speak up or can't. The voice of what was once the world's greatest superpower will be silent.

Barry: Ezekiel 38:13 mentions some nations that will protest the invasion of Israel, but not come to Israel's aid. There, we find the mention of Tarshish, which some people believe is a reference to Great Britain. And the "young lions" mentioned in that verse is believed by some to include America, which is an "offspring" of Britain. But this is highly unlikely. If you're familiar with the story of Jonah, you know that the prophet took a ship to Tarshish in an effort to avoid God's command that he preach to the Ninevites. Geographically, Jonah's escape route would place Tarshish somewhere in the Mediterranean, not in the Atlantic Ocean, where Great Britain is located.

The United States is not one of the young lions of "Sheba, Dedan, [or] the merchants or Tarshish" (Ezekiel 38:13). Tarshish was probably in Cyprus, or may have been in Spain. Sheba and Dedan are the regions now known as Saudi Arabia and the Arab Gulf states. These nations are currently establishing a relationship with Israel while, at the same time, the US is pulling away. So when the Ezekiel 38 war takes place, Saudi Arabia and the Arab Gulf states will object, saying, "Have you come to take plunder? Have you gathered your army to take booty, to carry away silver and gold, to take away livestock and goods, to take great plunder?" (verse 13). But we see no indication that anyone will come to Israel's help.

So the US is not in Bible prophecy. If it still exists during the end times, it will be among the nations that gather against Jerusalem near the end of the tribulation, as foretold in Zechariah 12:3.

4. Does the pandemic have any prophetic implications?

Barry: Without question the pandemic has prophetic implications, and the consequences go well beyond the obvious "pestilences" that

Jesus mentioned in Matthew 24:7 when He taught about the end times. The pandemic has polarized humanity like nothing else in history. It has broken families, divided countries, and created unprecedented levels of distrust in government officials and various leaders.

The prophetic aspect of this is that people have now been prepared for turning on each other during the tribulation. Those who do not bow to the antichrist and take his mark on the hand or forehead will be viewed by society as enemies of the greater good and will be executed for their beliefs. We have seen calls for strict punishments on those who, for whatever reason, are not open to taking vaccines, and we have seen restrictions placed on people's ability to buy and sell or to do business based on whether they have the proper vaccination credentials.

The list of consequences goes on and on. While the Bible does not say there will be a pandemic in the days right before the rapture, we can look at the actions of the antichrist and the mindset society will need to have if they want to survive under him. We know that people will either have to go along with his plans and to bow and worship him, or reject him. Those who do the latter will suffer. We are already seeing our world polarized along the lines of those who will cooperate with government mandates and those who won't, which is exactly what will happen during the end times. That means that the moment we are all waiting for—"in the twinkling of an eye" (1 Corinthians 15:52)—cannot be too far off!

Amir: There is no doubt the pandemic has had prophetic implications. Regardless of which side Christians fall on regarding the vaccine, most are against mandates. It's the *mandates* that have the prophetic element to them. For a government to force people to obey its directives under the guise of the greater good of humanity describes how the antichrist will function. The path we are on will eventually take us to the ultimate government mandate, which is that people will need to take the mark or die.

Another prophetic element to all this is that more and more, people are being forced to depend on the government if they want to survive. The socialist perspective of government is spreading, which advocates the idea that the government will take care of us if we do what it says. Many people are enamored by the idea of letting the government take care of their needs. Yet all we have to do is look at places like Venezuela and Cuba to realize that socialism doesn't work.

This is all part of the growing delusion of the last days that will lead to the strong deception that will occur during the tribulation—a deception that leads to widespread acceptance of the antichrist as the ruler of the world. Things are escalating in that direction, just as Jesus said they would when He spoke about the labor pains or sorrows that will build up as we approach the last days (Matthew 24:8). Jesus warned that there would be wars and rumors of wars, national and ethnic tensions, famines, pestilences, earthquakes, and weather-related events (verses 6-7). Events are unfolding in a way that will make it easier for the antichrist to implement his agenda when he arrives on the world scene.

Things are wrapping up quickly, and our redemption is drawing near. Make sure that you and those around you are ready for when the trumpet of God sounds, with the voice of an archangel, and tells us it's time to go home.

NOTES

1. This chapter opening was excerpted and adapted from portions of a booklet by Amir Tsarfati, *The Miracle Called Israel* (Eugene, OR: Harvest House, 2020).

2. "Israel Miracle? Gaza Strip Hamas Complain, 'Their God Changes The Paths Of Our Rockets Mid-Air,'" *news24*, July 23, 2014, https://www.news24.com/News24/Israel-Miracle-Gaza-Strip -Hamas-Complain-Their-God-Changes-The-Paths-Of-Our-Rockets-In-Mid-Air-20140722.

3. This chapter opening was excerpted and adapted from Amir Tsarfati, *Israel and the Church* (Eugene, OR: Harvest House, 2021), 37-38, 42.

4. This chapter opening was excerpted and adapted from portions of Amir Tsarfati with Dr. Rick Yohn, *Revealing Revelation* (Eugene, OR: Harvest House, 2022), 71-72, and Amir Tsarfati, *The Day Approaching* (Eugene, OR: Harvest House, 2020), 148-149.

5. This chapter opening was excerpted and adapted from Amir Tsarfati, *Israel and the Church* (Eugene, OR: Harvest House, 2021), 55, 93-94, 184.

6. This chapter opening was excerpted and adapted from portions of Amir Tsarfati, *The Day Approaching* (Eugene, OR: Harvest House, 2020), 169, 171, 189.

7. This chapter opening was excerpted and adapted from portions of Amir Tsarfati, *The Day Approaching* (Eugene, OR: Harvest House, 2020), 207-208.

8. This chapter opening was excerpted and adapted from portions of Amir Tsarfati with Dr. Rick Yohn, *Revealing Revelation* (Eugene, OR: Harvest House, 2022), 240, 245.

9. This chapter opening was excerpted and adapted from portions of Amir Tsarfati, *The Day Approaching* (Eugene, OR: Harvest House, 2020), 15-16, 23.

OTHER GREAT
HARVEST HOUSE BOOKS
BY AMIR TSARFATI

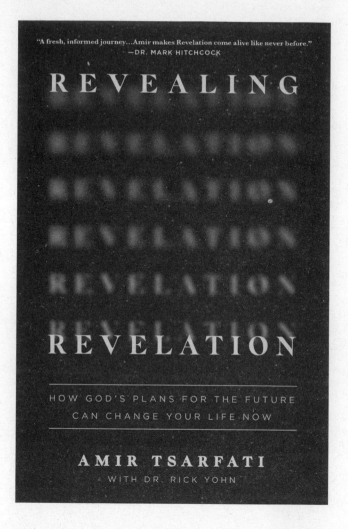

REVEALING

REVELATION

HOW GOD'S PLANS FOR THE FUTURE CAN CHANGE YOUR LIFE NOW

AMIR TSARFATI

WITH DR. RICK YOHN

Amir Tsarfati, with Dr. Rick Yohn, examines what Revelation makes known about the end times and beyond. Guided by accessible teaching that lets Scripture speak for itself, you'll see what lies ahead for every person in the end times—either in heaven or on earth. Are *you* ready?

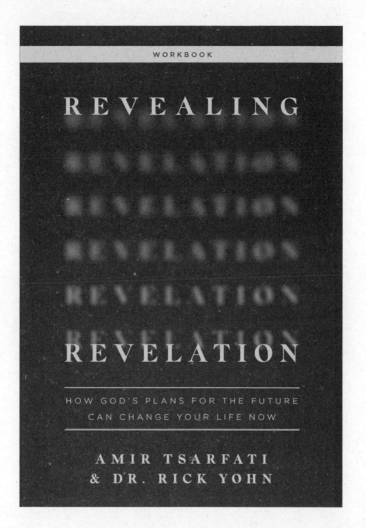

WORKBOOK

REVEALING

REVELATION

HOW GOD'S PLANS FOR THE FUTURE
CAN CHANGE YOUR LIFE NOW

AMIR TSARFATI
& DR. RICK YOHN

This companion workbook to *Revealing Revelation*—the product of many years of careful research—offers you a clear and exciting overview of God's perfect plan for the future. Inside you'll find principles from the Bible that equip you to better interpret the end-times signs, as well as insights about how Bible prophecy is relevant to your life today.

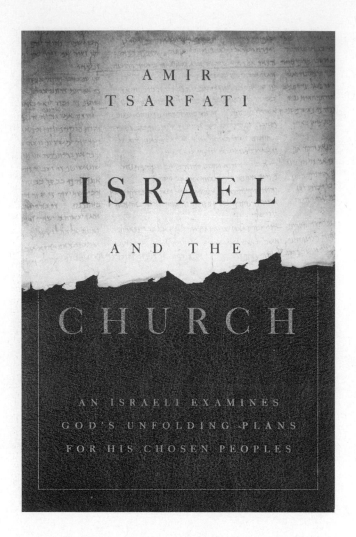

AMIR
TSARFATI

ISRAEL

AND THE

CHURCH

AN ISRAELI EXAMINES
GOD'S UNFOLDING PLANS
FOR HIS CHOSEN PEOPLES

In *Israel and the Church*, bestselling author and native Israeli Amir Tsarfati helps readers recognize the distinct contemporary and future roles of both the Jewish people and the church, and how together they reveal the character of God and His perfect plan of salvation.

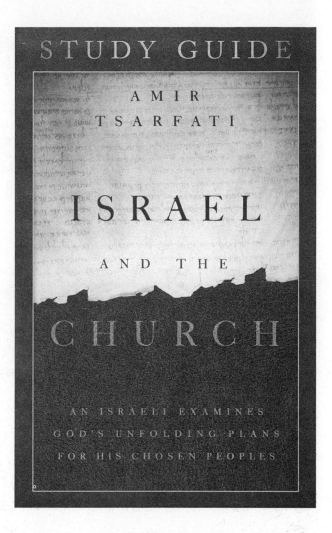

STUDY GUIDE

AMIR
TSARFATI

ISRAEL

AND THE

CHURCH

AN ISRAELI EXAMINES
GOD'S UNFOLDING PLANS
FOR HIS CHOSEN PEOPLES

To fully grasp what God has in store for the future, it's vital to understand His promises to Israel. The *Israel and the Church Study Guide* will help you do exactly that, equipping you to explore the Bible's many revelations about what is yet to come.

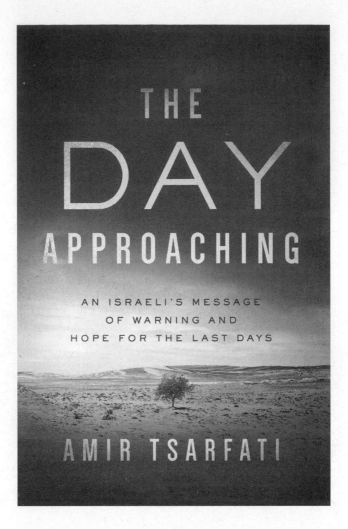

THE
DAY
APPROACHING

AN ISRAELI'S MESSAGE
OF WARNING AND
HOPE FOR THE LAST DAYS

AMIR TSARFATI

As a native Israeli of Jewish roots, Amir Tsarfati provides a distinct perspective that weaves biblical history, current events, and Bible prophecy together to shine light on the mysteries about the end times. In *The Day Approaching*, he points to the scriptural evidence that the return of the Lord is imminent.

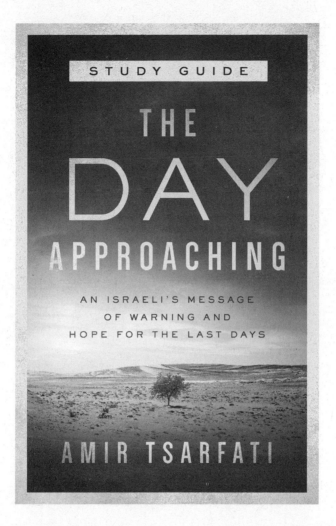

Jesus Himself revealed the signs that will alert us to the nearness of His return. In *The Day Approaching Study Guide*, you'll have the opportunity to take an up-close look at what those signs are, as well as God's overarching plans for the future, and how those plans affect you today.

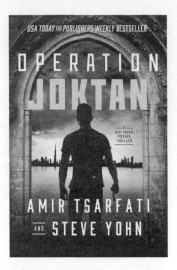

Amir Tsarfati with Steve Yohn
The Nir Tavor Mossad Thriller Series
Book One

"It was the perfect day—until the gunfire."

Nir Tavor is an Israeli secret service operative turned talented Mossad agent.

Nicole le Roux is a model with a hidden skill.

A terrorist attack brings them together, and then work forces them apart—until they're unexpectedly called back into each other's lives.

But there's no time for romance. As violent radicals threaten chaos across the Middle East, the two must work together to stop these extremists, pooling Nicole's knack for technology and Nir's adeptness with on-the-ground missions. Each heart-racing step of their operation gets them closer to the truth—and closer to danger.

In this thrilling first book in a new series, authors Amir Tsarfati and Steve Yohn draw on true events as well as tactical insights Amir learned from his time in the Israeli Defense Forces. For believers in God's life-changing promises, *Operation Joktan* is a suspense-filled page-turner that illuminates the blessing Israel is to the world.

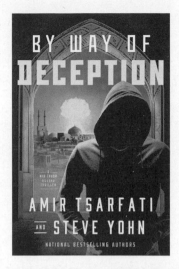

Book Two

The Mossad has uncovered Iran's plans to smuggle untraceable weapons of mass destruction into Israel. The clock is ticking, and agents Nir Tavor and Nicole le Roux can't act quickly enough.

Nir and Nicole find themselves caught in a whirlwind plot of assassinations, espionage, and undercover recon, fighting against the clock to stop this threat against the Middle East. As they draw closer to danger—and closer to each other—they find themselves ensnared in a lethal web of secrets. Will they have to sacrifice their own lives to protect the lives of millions?

Inspired by real events, authors Amir Tsarfati and Steve Yohn reteam for this suspenseful follow-up to the bestselling *Operation Joktan*. Filled with danger, romance, and international intrigue, this Nir Tavor thriller reveals breathtaking true insights into the lives and duties of Mossad agents—and delivers a story that will have you on the edge of your seat.